The
Mysteries Of
Self-Belief

SB
SELF-BELIEF

66

*If the belief you have in yourself fails,
everything around you and what you do will
also fail.*

The *Mysteries Of Self-Belief*

Discover the Mystical Power in you for Greatness

RICHMOND GEORGE AHORNOR

ISBN: 978-9988-54-034-0

Published by:
Kees & Geyts Media Solutions
P. O. Box MP 4147, Mamprobi-Accra
keesandgeyts@gmail.com
+233272434748

Cover & Layout Design by:
Supa Authentic Creations
+233273017457

Printed by:
Kees & Geyts Media Solutions
+233272434748

For your personal copy of this book or bulk purchase please contact the author on +233 273017457 or
Email: georgeahornor@yahoo.com

Dedication

To my great biological father, the late George Ahornor Snr., an extraordinary entrepreneur. One of the successful businessmen who ever lived and an inspiration to everyone who knew him.

I only wish you were here to read this book.
You left us all too soon.

Acknowledgement

I am highly indebted to God Almighty for preparing me for a season like this. I personally believe that no accomplishment in life is without the help of many known and unknown individuals who have directly or indirectly impacted our lives.

My heartfelt gratitude goes to all who have championed and hailed with great enthusiasm as this book was birthed. You were the ones who believed it is of great importance that, this book is written so as to show others how to believe in themselves, be who they were meant to be and manifest the greatness they possess.

As a result of a lifetime dedicated learning and personal development, this book is a collective contribution of many mentors, teachers, role models, friends and family. Your footprints are forever within this book of guidance and inspiration on self-belief.

Contents

Preface

I strongly believe to be successful, you must first believe in yourself. Be productive, yearn to do more, think more and have a positive perspective about everything you do and go beyond your call of duty. This book is set to strengthen people who believe in themselves and want to attain more with their self-belief. Basically, it is also for people who lack self-belief and don't realize the mysteries and power behind their beliefs.

The revelations and mysteries contained in the pages ahead will boost your productivity and your way of thinking. It will influence the way you behave, for you to work hard in getting all you want and the most important things to you. For the past four years, I have spoken more than 16 times before audiences as many as 1,824 at maximum and 8 at minimum about self-belief. In every case, I have always focused on boosting the confidence in people as well as helping them discover their self-worth, maximize their untapped potential and unveiling the secrets to what self-belief can help one to attain.

If I was only given 2 minutes to speak to you, I could only convey one thought that would help you get all you want in life. I would tell you to believe in yourself first and your capabilities has no limitations. You can achieve all you want in life. I happened to have a chat with a group of successful young men in Accra Airport City, talking about experiences and their driving factors. All of them were successful businessmen but, were both humble and grateful. As we discussed the reasons why they had managed to achieve so much in life. From what they said, the common factor was *"success begins with self-belief"* they started believing they could and the rest was commentary.

This piece is dedicated to helping you recapture the importance and mysteries of your true self and accompanying a positive mental attitude which will manifest the success you seek.

Foreword

My son in the Lord, Richmond George Ahornor has used this exposition as a means of giving clarity to the word *belief,* which most often is undervalued and underestimated. Anyone who has ever accomplished anything out of the ordinary most often turns out to have done so out of self-belief. When you develop your self-belief, a character of self motivation is created which produces a drive for achievement without external influences.

With self-belief, you become a different person in every part of your work, life and career. Self-belief creates a natural stimulus that drives boldness, creativity and extreme imagination which causes you to take risk and explore where others without self-belief will not dare. You would be willing to consider unusual and risky alternatives and to commit yourself wholeheartedly to projects that are only sitting today on the back burner of your mind.

With self-belief, nothing would be impossible, for you. More than anything else you would feel terrific about yourself. You'll also feel happy about every part of your life. Knowing deep down inside that you have the ability to take whatever steps and make whatever changes, necessary to assure that your life is exactly the way you want it. Richmond always says ***"Self-belief is the heartbeat of success."*** By reading this book, your self-belief will be awaken and your life will be successful. God bless you.

—PROPHET JAMES OWUSU
General Overseer
(True Light Worship Centre)

Introduction

"Self-Belief is the heartbeat of success" – Richmond George Ahornor

Famous motivational speaker, Brian Tracy said and I agree with him, *"your life is hugely determined by yourself as a result of your own choices and decisions. Whatever be your outcome from these choices, they are the results of what you did or perhaps what you failed to do"*. Therefore, your chances of success and anything you try is *self-centered*.

Throughout and after high school, I always strive to find my purpose and master in my chosen field. I became so curious and wanted to know more about life. I was able to discover self-belief as a strong weapon and I began researching to know more about it. From my research and personal experience, I discovered that whatever has happened to me in the past, present and future. I am responsible for the consequences of even listening to people's opinion and the outcome thereof. Everything said in this book, were not just written out of the blues or by hypothetical imaginations. But practical life experience, years of research, contributions of great people and practical application of the hidden mystery.

The very best way to predict your life and your chances of success, is to believe in yourself. Right now, everybody in the world have the desire to be healthy, happy, famous, rich and successful in anything they do. But the only way for you to attain all is for you to first believe in yourself that it is possible. *"Self-belief is the first step to personal success." – Richmond George Ahornor*

If you cannot believe in yourself, no one will believe in you. The only way I was able to make people believe in me and my capabilities was to live a life trusting in myself. You should take advantage of the mysteries behind your belief. It is one of the greatest keys to achieving all you want.

Join me on a journey to discover and explore the vast, uncharted regions of your own hidden ability. Because of the importance of this mental attitude, this book will help you believe in yourself and release your inner powers. Decide today to believe in yourself.

Chapter One

The Concept of Self-Belief

"If the belief you have in yourself fails, everything around you and what you do will also fail" – Richmond George Ahornor

Wow! I'm thrilled and pumped; I wake up every day convinced of one truth that I'm an asset to my generation. It is so clear in my mind and has been hunting me not to fail and give up on my purpose. If everyone would be able to see how great they are in their minds, they would literally astonish themselves. Whenever your belief is at work, your performance is in view. If you can see what you are capable of doing and take bold steps to do whatever you set your mind at doing, you would be very successful at anything you try. Success is only limited to people who believe in themselves. The resting place of your belief is your mind. Your mind is the centre of your life and also the centre of your decisions and actions. If you can see it in your mind then you can have it in your hands. Therefore, you don't believe what you see but rather you see what you believe. Everyone wants a short-cut and often times people ask ***"tell me your secret or tell me the keys".*** By default, everyone in the world right now wants to be happy, successful or famous. So in the quest to be happy or successful, people try different ways and means to get what they want. At some point in life, some give up their quest and others end up going the wrong path to get what they want. It is only a few people who are able to succeed.

If success was just a joy ride, everyone would be happy and successful. This is not only about how to be successful, but how to master a hidden ability that is free, which will help you become successful in anything you do. I am not only stressing on self-belief, religious beliefs or how to be successful but I am also stressing on how to use your self-belief to achieve greatness and all that you want. This is because self-belief is the most important tool for greatness. After years of exploring my beliefs, I found out that, until you realize that everything that happens to you is in your own hands and you are therefore responsible for your own actions, you will never be successful.

Mostly, we do hear about belief, self-belief and so on and so forth. Some people suggest things like hard work, discipline, persistence, focus and the rest but these are all by-products of something else that we can all develop. We demonstrate the belief we have in ourselves in a number of ways; our behaviour, our mood and even how we carry ourselves. It's common for individuals who lack self-belief to find certain areas of their life affected. Relationships can break down, careers can stale, lifestyle can become unbalanced and a positive state of mind can be undermined unless some action is taken to improve these qualities. When you believe in yourself, you hold yourself to impossible standards. Belief—a simple word but misunderstood, however, if you are going to really change, you have to move from ***an opinion to a belief and a belief to a conviction and a conviction into an action.***

Your Beliefs

"The only thing that stands between a man and what he wants from life is often merely, the will to try it and the faith to believe that it is possible" – Richard M. DeVos

Beliefs have been generally defined as inward convictions, a feeling of certainty about what something means. A belief is both mental and emotional. It is rooted in the mind and in the heart. When you believe in a cause, you fight for it and when you believe in your religion, you live it. Moreover, when you believe in others, you support and uplift them. **Beliefs drive us.** They are at the root of all purpose and all actions. This is to say, your beliefs will dictate your action.

A belief is also a feeling and a mindset of absolute certainty. Before anything in this world was achieved, created or invented, there was certainty. If you want to achieve anything in life, you need to be certain that you will achieve it. Beliefs control results, because you will never take action towards something you don't believe is possible. You can have all the education, but it doesn't matter. If you don't believe you can do it, you will never do it. Do you think Michael Jordan could have become the greatest if he didn't believe in himself? No way, Never! He would have quit when things got hard. He would have quit when he was dropped from his high school basketball team. How about Serena Williams? Do you think she would be the greatest female tennis player in history without belief? The great athletes, entrepreneurs, great people, whomever you can think or imagine of would never have become great without belief. They are all great because they believed in themselves. They believed when no one else did. They believed when they were rejected and people said they were no good. They believe when they were at the rock bottom and people said it's not possible for them. This is your dream and you will succeed maybe not immediately but absolutely and definitely that has to be your foundational mindset. It is the power of belief that causes things to happen in our lives.

Understanding Belief

"If you believe you can do a thing, or you believe you cannot, in either case, you are probably right." – Henry Ford

I got a better insight about the word belief when I read a book by John Milton Fogg, which gave me an incredible understanding into the word *belief*. English is so weak when it comes to defining the true meaning and origin of a word because it loses its natural identity or meaning after translation. But when you study the root of the word belief you gain a greater understanding of its depth and meaning. The true definition of belief will teach you why our beliefs are so powerful.

The word belief comes from two words thus *Be* and *lief*. **Be** comes from being, which is a state of existence. The process of living is being. Therefore, to be; is to live. The second word **lief** comes from the Indo-European word **leubh** which means—love which has been translated to English as *beloved, valued or willing*. So when you put that together, it changes the entire idea of the word belief. ***Belief means to be in love with.*** Belief doesn't mean you have to know for a fact, all you have to do is love it. It takes a concrete knowledge, which is a mental process and changes it into love. Which is a function of the heart. A true belief is something that resonates both in heart and mind. When you believe in someone else; your spouse, a friend, whomever, what you are really saying is you love them.

Let me give you an example. Most researchers would say that less than 8% of the population writes down their goals. Why is that? Most likely it is because they didn't believe with absolute certainty they would attain them. Have you avoided writing down your goals? If so, what kind of damaging message are you giving yourself? ***"Goals not written are only a wish."*** What if instead of having unshakable conviction, all you had to do was to be in love with your goals. Love the idea, love what they stand for, what they would do for you, and simply be in love with them. If you love them, you will act. Not only will you act, you will also attract all that you believe into your life. James Allen wrote, ***"The soul attracts that which it secretly harbours; that which it loves."*** It is a liberating concept! In my life there are a lot of things that I love, and because of that I believe in them.

The Law of Belief

The law of belief has proven to be the most important mental law essential for personal success which makes self-belief as a state of mind or a mentality for success. This law says, ***"Whatever you believe with conviction, becomes your reality."*** It means that whatever you subconsciously feel to be true in your inner world (thoughts) long enough, will always show up in your outer world (experience). Once you start to better understand this law you'll see that this is very obvious. Everyone actually views their world through a lens of beliefs, attitudes, prejudices and preconceived notions. Brian Tracy wrote, ***"Your beliefs are a product of your thought, your thoughts creates your convictions, your convictions creates your attitude, your attitude controls your perception and your perception dictates your behaviour."*** The heart of success is self-belief, your attitude, mind-set and action. And you will need these key components for personal success.

From the Bible, ***"As a man thinketh in his heart, so is he."*** (Proverbs 23:7) This means that, you always act on the outside based on your innermost beliefs and convictions about yourself. The same Bible in the New Testament—Jesus says, ***"According to your faith, it is done unto you."*** (Matthew 9:29) This is another way of saying that your intense beliefs become your realities. They determine what happens to you. Dr. William James of Harvard said in 1905, ***"Belief creates its verification in fact."*** He went on to say, *"The greatest revolution of my generation is the discovery that individuals, by changing their inner attitudes of mind, can change the outer aspects of their lives."*

What Is Self-Belief?

From the above definition of belief, I am convinced you have caught an insight on the meaning of self-belief. If basically, belief means *to be in love with* then self-belief means **to be in love with yourself.** Self-belief is a mystical power which exist within each one of us. I see self-belief as the trust in our capability to see and withstand the challenges that life hits us. It goes a long way to give us a feeling of being worthy, justifiable, permitted to state our needs and wants and to enjoy the fruits of our efforts. Self-belief is a way of life, not religion but a state of mind which determines one's attitude. It always stems from positive mindset, relationships, perspective and ways of doing things. To me, self-belief emerges to be the mother of self-confidence, self-worth, self-esteem or self-image. If you lack any of these you will never be successful or happy with life. Money cannot buy self-belief therefore you need to have it; it's a necessity for personal growth.

The dictionary defines self-belief as confidence in your own abilities or judgment. And the same dictionary defines confidence as freedom from doubt; belief in yourself and your abilities. These definitions sums up to one thing which is believe in one's self. It is very important to believe in yourself. When I told one of my uncles in Amsterdam about this book; he asked me, *so what is self-belief?* I remember telling him; ***self-belief is the heartbeat of personal success.*** If you want to be successful at anything you do, you have to believe it's possible. And you will achieve what you want, no matter the circumstance you may find yourself right now or at a point in life.

Self-belief is a self-motivating mindset, even if you receive a bad remark, you use it to motivate yourself that you can improve and do better. After saying these words, my uncle then asked me, is self-belief not pride? I smiled and said *"No papa! Not at all, it is only an unsecured person, who would mistake self-belief for pride."* Believing yourself has to do with accepting yourself as you are and be your biggest fan even if no one is following. It builds your confidence and makes you brave. I agree with the King of Pop, Michael Jackson when he said; ***"I don't care if the whole world is against you or teasing you or saying you're not going to make it. Believe in yourself, no matter*** *what."* I want to destroy your unbelief with a powerful scripture. In the book of Mark 9:23 ***"Jesus said to him, if you can believe; all things are possible to him who believes."*** To this extent, I do not know of anything you cannot do or accomplish with self-belief.

Self-Belief Is A Necessity For Every Soul

Throughout life, self-belief makes a vital contribution. It is a strong tool that every living soul needs. The rate at which self-belief affects our lives can never be undermined. It provides strength, resistance to fear and capacity for regeneration. We can never grow psychologically if we lack self-belief. When self-belief is present, the adversities of life becomes diminished. Instead of striving to have the desire to manifest joy, we tend to be more influenced by the desire to avoid pain and difficulty. We shall always be frightened in this world, if we do not believe in ourselves nor our efficiency or goodness.

Psychology, Technology & The Future

Due to rapid change, there's been a shift from a manufacturing society to an information society, the shift from physical labour to mind-work as the dominant employee activity. Science and technology has experienced a massive breakthrough and an unprecedented level of competitiveness. Which has created demands for higher levels of education and training than were required of previous generations. These rapid change forms new demands on our psychological resources.

Specifically, these developments ask for a greater capacity for innovation, self-management, personal responsibility, and self-direction. Today, organizations need not only an unprecedented higher level of knowledge and skill among all those who participate, but also a higher level of personal autonomy, self-reliance, self-trust, and the capacity to exercise initiative—in one word, self-belief. This means that people possessing a decent level of self-belief are now required economically in large numbers. In essence, this is a new phenomenon.

Your Mind Is A Powerful Tool

The mind is the most powerful force in the universe. Like every other species capable of awareness, we depend for our survival and well-being on the guidance of our distinctive form of consciousness. Which is uniquely human, our conceptual faculty—the faculty of abstraction, generalization, and integration. This form of consciousness is what I understand by the term mind. In essence, our ability to reason, which means to grasp relationships. Our lives and well-being depend on the appropriate exercise of our minds. Mind is more than immediate explicit awareness. It is a complex architecture of structures and processes. It includes more than the verbal, linear, analytic processes. It includes the totality of mental life, including the subconscious, the intuitive, and the symbolic. The mind serves as a platform, through which we reach out to and apprehend the world.

Your Thoughts

"There's nothing either good or bad, but thinking makes it so."
- William Shakespeare

I am without doubt that, thought can change the surface of the entire planet—in essence, our thought is the source of all things in the world and without it there would be no modern conveniences. In fact, there would be no advance over life from primitive ages.

Your character and everything about your life is determined by your thoughts. Your reality is as a result of your thoughts, they are creative. Your thought can make or break you. When you realize that there can be no action or reaction, either good or bad, without the generating force of thought initiating it, then comes the Biblical saying *"As a man thinketh in his heart, so is he."* Sir James Jeans an English physicist, astronomer and mathematician suggested that the universe was merely a creation that resulted from the thought of some great universal mind. I believe the universe was created by God and He did this by his thought.

"We become what we habitually contemplate." — George Russell

You must keep in mind that many of the thoughts you think are not yours at all, you're not the author of all thought and there are other things that influences and generates your thoughts. The thought of others, through what we hear in conversations, books, radio, newspapers, the songs we listen to and the movies we watch are all major influences among others. Some of them are very helpful to us as they harmonize with our innermost thoughts and create a way to greater visions in our lives. Inversely, these thoughts can be upsetting and destroys our self-belief system. It mislead us from higher purposes in life. These external sources can be trouble makers. Moreover, it is true that hard work alone cannot earn you success. This world is filled with people who have worked hard but have little to show for it. Something more than hard work is necessary— namely, creative thinking and firm belief in your ability to execute your ideas. Higher achievers of society in history have succeeded through their thinking. Their hands were merely helpers to their brains. Another important factor, your desire must be an all-obsessing one, your thoughts and aims can be coordinated and your energy be concentrated and applied without letup. It may be that you want riches, fame, position, knowledge or power as everyone has their own idea of success. But whatever you consider to be your idea or meaning about success you can have your objective provided you are willing to make it the burning desire of your life.

The Magic of Believing - Merlin

There was a young man who dreamed of becoming a knight for King Arthur's Knight of the Round Table. Before he could become a knight, he had to pass one last test—he has to slay a dragon. He was scared to death. He asked one of the knights what he should do about his tremendous fear. This knight advised him to see Merlin the Magician because he had a magic sword. When the young man told Merlin about his problem. Merlin went to his back room and brought out a beautiful, gilded sword. Merlin then instructed him, *"This sword is magic and the day you go out to slay your dragon, come see me and I will give you this magic sword. But make sure that your scabbard is empty. And remember this, the sword only works its magic if you are in danger."*

One week later, the would-be knight returned. He was dressed for battle and as Merlin instructed, his scabbard was empty. As Merlin went to the back room again, he told the young man to close his eyes. Then Merlin returned and put the sword into his scabbard. As the young man left, He reminded him, *"This sword will only work its magic if you are in danger."* The young man now more confident, rode his horse out onto the plains where he confronted his dragon.

The Fierce Battle

It was a fierce battle, the dragon was breathing fire. The dragon's tail knocked the young man off his trusty steed. The young man was on the ground and the dragon came in for the kill. Just at that moment, the young man remembered about the magic sword, he took the sword out of his scabbard and started slashing the dragon's legs. The dragon was hurt and fell down. The young man jumped onto the dragon and put the sword into the dragon's heart and killed the dragon. The young man returned home victorious. The first person he went to see was Merlin. He told Merlin about how the magic sword saved his life.

As he took it out of his scabbard to return it, he looked it in amazement. *"Merlin this isn't the same sword you showed me last week. This isn't the beautiful, gilded magic sword. It's just as ordinary sword!"* Merlin nodded and said, *"There is no magic sword. The magic is believing."* After reading this story I was left in amazement and got this simple axiom—***"Whatever you believe in, works for you."*** The young man believed the magic sword could save his life, therefore, he believed in its ability to kill the dragon. He saw the ordinary sword as a magic sword. There's a lot of depth in this story.

Whatever You Believe In, Works For You

If you can believe in yourself and believe that you are a magic being, strong with supernatural powers and can therefore, achieve or have all you want then you will really get them. It's so simple but it's not easy. How many of us see ourselves in a different way even if no one is seeing something good in us. Can we still see greatness in ourselves? You are an ordinary human being, and it was also an ordinary sword; but what made it so different or perhaps gave it a supernatural ability? What makes you special, or gives you a special skill or gift to be great? It's the mindset—your belief in yourself and his believe in the sword. Where your believe stops that's where your adventure stops. I strongly believe; Steve Jobs, Bill Gates, Cristiano Ronaldo, Warren Buffet, Kofi Annan, Serena Williams, Jeff Bezos, Aliko Dangote, Ruth Porat, Kwame Despite, Oprah Winfrey, Mark Zuckerberg and any other successful person you know did not become successful with magic, occult or whatever you can call it. But they started believing they can and believed they have a potential, mind or gift and they used it to become very successful.

No one in this world, who is successful today will tell you self-belief is not part of his or her keys to success. Luka Modric on winning his first Ballon d'Or, when asked about his secret to success, he never denied self-belief. Belief—it's a way of life, it's part of you, in your mind and it creates a mental picture of the success you desire. The way you see things, the way you understand and approach situations in your life are mostly based on your beliefs and it goes a long way to decide your choices when making decisions.

You will agree with me that, history is replete with famous people whose belief in a concept or a cause drove them without question to accomplish remarkable things. Martin Luther King Jr. had a dream (a belief) that one day all people would have the same freedom in the United States, and that belief drove him to fight for change. It dictated his actions. Another example is Nelson Mandela of South Africa who had a life struggle against the Apartheid in South Africa and not forgetting Dr. Kwame Nkrumah of Ghana, both of them were willing to suffer because of their passion and belief they had for freedom. You can also think of Mohandas Gandhi and his belief in a free society in India. He gave his life for the cause he believed in. He is famous for saying, ***"Be the change you wish to see in the world."*** Those are not just words to him.

Limiting Beliefs

Unfortunately, while beliefs can be very empowering they can be equally disempowering. Often times our beliefs are negative, or pessimistic about a person, situation, even ourselves, and they limit us and sabotage our results. It is important to stop and take time to analyse your beliefs. Are they helping or hindering? Do they move you forward or hold you back? Successful people think differently and believe differently than the average person. These beliefs that they adopt, lay the foundation for the level of success they experience. You see, beliefs are not necessarily what's true or factual in the real world. The power of each belief comes only from the individual believer. That is to say; you can believe whatever you want to believe. As long as you believe it to be true, it will be true in your life. Consequently, you will attract events, experiences and people in your life to match your beliefs. For this reason, it is crucial to adopt only the beliefs that serve you and to let go of those beliefs that limit you.

The Lion Who Thought He Was A Sheep

There is this famous story about a lion who grew among herds of sheep and believed he was one of them which I know you might have heard it or familiar with it. There has been different versions of the story over the past years but I think in relation to the main context this is the best version that I want to share with you. In a village lived an old shepherd. One faithful morning, he took his sheep out to feed and while they were grazing, he suddenly heard an unusual noise coming from a blotch of grass which first sounded like a kitten. Led by his curiosity, the old shepherded went to see what was the source of this insistent sound and to his surprise he found a lone shuddering lion cub. He left the area quickly after discovering what it was, having in mind the danger he would be in if the mother returns and watched from a distance to see if the mother lion would return. Nevertheless, after the sun began to set and there was still no signs of the mother lion returning, he then decided to take the lion cub to his farm house for safety and survival.

The Lion Lost His True Self

Over the next 8 months, the old shepherd hand fed this cub with fresh milk and kept him warm, safe and secure in the protective confines of the farm house. After the cub had grown into a playful, energetic ball of shiny muscle, he would take him out daily with the sheep to graze. He started going out in the fields, playing with the sheep, playing with the lambs. The lion kept growing with the sheep and became a part of the herd. They accepted him as one of their own and he acted like one of them. After 15 months had passed the lion cub had become an adult lion but he acted, sounded, responded and behaved just like one of the sheep (He would bleat like a sheep, he'd eat grass like a sheep). In essence, the lion had become a sheep by association. He had lost himself and became one of them.

One hot day, the shepherded sat on a rock, taking refuge in the slight shade of a leafless tree, he watch over his flock as they waded into the quiet flowing water of a river to drink. The lion who thought he was a sheep followed them into the water to drink. Suddenly, just across the river there appeared out of the thick jungle bush a large beast that the lion cub had never seen before. The sheep panicked and, as if under the spell of some survival instinct. Leaped out of the water and dashed out of the water towards into the direction of the farm. They never stopped until they were all safely huddled behind the fence of the pen. Strangely the lion cub who was now a grown lion also huddled with them striking with fear. While the flock scrambles for the safety of the farm, the beast made a sound that seem to shake the forest. When the shepherd lifted his head above the tall grass, the shepherd could see that the beast held in his blood drench mouth the lifeless body of a lamp from the flock. The man knew that danger has returned to his part of the forest.

The Lion Discovers His True Self

Seven days passed without further incidence and then while the flock grazed the lion went down to the river to drink. As he burnt over the water he suddenly panics and run wildly towards the farm house for safety. The sheep did not run and wondered why he had. While the lion wondered why the sheep had not run since he had seen the beast again. After a while, the young lion went slowly back to the flock and then to the water to drink again. Once more, he saw the beast and froze in panic. It was his own reflection in the water. While he tried to understand what he was seeing, suddenly the beast appeared out of the jungle again, the flock dashed with break neck speed towards the farm house but before the young lion could move, the beast stepped in the water toward him and made that deafening sound that fell the forest. For a moment, the young lion felt that his life was about to end. He realised that, he saw not just one beast, but two, one in the water and one before him. His head was spinning with confusion as the beast came within 10ft of him and growled at him face to face with frightening power in a way that seem to say to him, *"try it, and come and follow me"*. He felt stirrings that he had never known before. As fear gripped the young lion, he decided to try to appease the beast and make the same sound.

However, the only noise that came from his gaping jaws was the sound of a sheep. The beast responded with an even louder burst that seemed to say, *"try it again."* After seven or eight attempts, the young lion suddenly heard himself made the same sound as the beast. He also felt stirrings in his body and feelings that he had never known before. It was as if he was experiencing a total transformation in mind, body and soul. Getting access to the keys to open the gates.

Total Transformation For The Lion
Suddenly, there stood in the river of life two beast growling at and to each other. Then the shepherd saw something he would never forget. As the beastly sounds filled the forest for miles around, the big beast stopped, turned his back on the young lion and started towards the forest. Then he paused and looked at the young lion and growled, as if to say *"are you coming?"* The young lion knew what the gesture meant and suddenly realized that his day of decision had arrived— the day he would have to choose whether to continue to live life as a sheep or to be the self he had just discovered.

He knew that, to become his true self, he would give up the safe, secured, predictable, and simple life of the farm and enter the frightening, wild, untamed, unpredictable, dangerous life of the jungle. It was a day to become true to himself and leave the false image of another life behind. It was invitation to a *"sheep"* to become the *"king of the jungle"*. Most importantly, it was **an invitation for the body of the lion to possess the spirit of a lion.** After looking back and forth at the farm and the jungle a few times, the lion turned his back on the farm and sheep with whom he had lived for years, and he followed the beast into the forest to become his true self—a lion king.

Discover Your True Self

"When a man finds himself, he finds freedom and all riches, achievements, and prosperity." – Claude M. Bristol

We must stand before the mirror of meaning and ask; why, having been endowed with the courageous heart of a lion, do we live as sheep? The lion's mirror of meaning was the water that revealed his true self. When I read this fantastic story, I became overwhelmed with deep insight comparing to the lives of many in this generation. Not knowing who we really are because of the family, society or country perhaps association that we were born and raised from. This has created a limitation to what we are. When you discover your true self, you release your inherent potential with you. The choice about your future is very important. In essence, you don't have to leave the choice of your true self into the hands of someone else—not even your parents or spouse. On your journey to discover and become your true self you would have to give up a lot of things. This will cost you but you have to be willing to sacrifice every comfort you have. Being in your comfort zone and never fighting for what and who you're is a trap. After the young lion discovered who he was, he made a decision out of fear with courage to go into the wild, dangerous forest and fight for his destiny.

Discovering your true self requires you to look back and assess your past and take a bold step forward believing you can and will survive. Sometimes we must ask ourselves why we waste much time sniffing at every distractions and why we tremble at the thought of revealing who we are to the world, and allowing ourselves into muddles of mediocrity and settling for scraps of reward when life has offered us unlimited ability to believe in ourselves, be creative and independent. If you are not ready to ascend to another level of existence and possess the spirit of your true self (greatness) then I don't know why you are here.

Chapter Two

Build Your Abilities

"The moment we believe that success is determined by an ingrained level of ability, we will be brittle in the face of adversity." – Josh Waitzkin

Before I talk about building your abilities, I want to talk about an American chess player who was able to believe in himself to build his abilities and dominate the history of chess and martial arts; in the person of Josh Waitzkin. He first caught a glimpse of a chess set while 6 years old and walking with his mother in New York City's Washington Square Park. From age 9 on, Josh dominated the US scholastic chess scene and till date, nobody has won the chess championship that Josh has but he did something different from chess. At twenty-one, Josh began to transition away from his early career in chess and into the study of the Chinese Martial Art, Tai Chi Chuan with Grandmaster William CC Chen. He realized that he has learnt how to grow in building his abilities and so he can apply that to other domains. He devoted himself relentlessly to Tai Chi. And after lots of hard work, many failures and broken joints he became a great martial artist and won 5 National Championship titles in the Middleweight, Light Heavyweight, and Heavyweight divisions.

Fixed Belief (Mindset) & Growth Belief

To build your abilities you need to discover and possess certain belief patterns or mindset. In relation to my main subject I use belief over mindset, either ways, though there may be some differences it meets at the same meaning. There is no doubt that your beliefs come from your habitual thinking patterns which is your mind and goes ahead to make up your mindset about yourself or something. Therefore, I am not wrong to use belief as mindset. It is known as fixed mindset and growth mindset which was discovered by Carol Dweck. With a fixed belief, people believe their qualities are fixed traits and therefore cannot change. These people document their intelligence and talents rather than working to develop and improve them. They also believe that, talent alone leads to success, and effort is not required.

Alternatively, in a growth belief people have an underlying belief that their learning and intelligence can grow with time and experience. When people believe they can get smarter, they realize that their effort has an effect on their success, so they put in extra time to go an extra mile, leading to higher achievement. This research was conducted by Carol Dweck of Stanford University and it is so true. According to Dweck, when a student has a fixed belief, they believe that their basic abilities, intelligence, and talents are fixed traits. They think that you are born with a certain amount and that's all you have.

People with a fixed belief always want to appear intelligent, because they believe that they were born with a fixed level of intelligence that cannot be modified. These people have a fear of looking dumb to people because they do not believe that they can redeem themselves once people look at them as being unintelligent.

In a growth belief, however, students believe their abilities and intelligence can be developed with effort, learning, and persistence. Their basic abilities are simply a starting point for their potential. They don't believe everyone is the same, but they hold true to the idea that everyone can become smarter if they are willing to try. Your fixed beliefs about you will hold you back from making positive change. If you have a trait that you believe cannot be changed, such as your intelligence, your weight, or your bad habits, you will avoid situations that could possibly be uncomfortable or that you think are useless.

One of the keys to success is not simply effort, focus or resilience but a growth belief. To fulfil our potentials we have to start thinking differently. We have to realize that we are not chained to our current capabilities. The brain is very malleable and we can change our own ability to think and to perform better. People with a fixed belief, their brain becomes most active when receiving information about how they perform such as a greater score, or achievement but the people with a growth belief, their brains becomes most active when receiving information about what they could do next time. In other words, people with a fixed belief worry about how they are judged but those with the growth belief focus on learning and performing better the next time. People with a fixed belief see effort as a bad thing whiles those with growth belief sees effort as what makes one smart and a way to grow. Setbacks, challenges and difficulties are part of growth to people with the growth belief.

The Challenge

In a study, children were given a puzzle to try. Some of the kids were praised like *"wow, you must be smart at this"* and to others they said *"you must have tried really hard"*. They asked the kids what kind of puzzle you would they like to try; the easy or difficult? Majority of the kids who were praised with a fixed belief said the easy one whiles the kids with the growth belief said the difficult one and in the end, they were given a difficult puzzle. Those with the fixed belief praise perform poorly and those with a growth belief improved in their performance and did well.

From this, we could conclude that the growth belief is always open to new challenge while they learn to improve on themselves and those with a fixed belief are only comfortable in their state of performance and hate new challenges. We should encourage schools to develop and instil a growth belief in children so they can grow and develop their abilities to help them believe in themselves and succeed, not only in school but beyond. Instead of feeling…learn and teach.

First, recognize that the growth belief is not only beneficial but it is also supported by science. When we work hard to improve ourselves the brain changes and become more capable. And we can grow by learning to teach others about how to develop their abilities. Also listen to your fixed belief voice and talk back with a growth belief voice. Whenever you hear *'I can't do it'* voice with your fixed belief add *'yet'*, therefore, ***'I can't do it yet, I will definitely'.*** This will help us fulfil our potentials and improve each day to become whatever we desire to be.

Develop A Growth Belief

To develop a growth belief you have to acknowledge and embrace your weaknesses. Maybe you know that you are lazy and tend to put things off until the last minute. Try to plan around that by making modest goals and giving yourself a reasonable amount of time to accomplish them. Here are some keys I discovered that will help you to develop a growth belief;

1. View Challenges as opportunities: We are constantly faced with important decisions, such as whether to accept a new job, or signing up to take a new class. Taking on these challenges is a big part of developing as a person. The more we challenge ourselves, the more opportunities we have to learn about ourselves. New challenges equal new opportunities. Embarking on a new challenge may be frightening due to the risk of failure. This may result in avoiding various challenges and continuing down the usual path, holding onto excuses that we tell ourselves so we can remain in our comfort zones. The truth is, staying in your comfort zone because you are scared to venture out can become uncomfortable. If you avoid challenges, you will not be provided with opportunities to learn and grow. Instead, you will be troubled by the sense that things are not just right.

2. Know your leaning style: Never underestimate the power of knowing your learning style and use the right learning strategies. If you are able to identify the best ways that you learn, you can optimize your time while researching or attending classes. Various learning styles can work together for people who have a growth belief. Learning styles allow you to blend and combine your own bits of intelligence into many different patterns. Learning styles relate to different learning approaches that you can find to be the most effective for yourself, so once these are identified, people can feel that their knowledge is expanding and they are getting better at what they are studying or learning new styles.

3. Your brain has the ability to change throughout life: It is proven that the human brain has the ability to change throughout life. Your brain forms new connections throughout life that allow it to make adjustments when you are faced with new situations or a new environment. Neuropsychiatric explains how your brain can be retrained and reorganized, showing that there is always room to grow. If you are aware that your brain is constantly changing, then you are more likely to adopt a growth belief. There's no doubt that, the brain is not fixed, which literally means that the mind is also not fixed either. Become a better student, leader or entrepreneur by embracing growth belief activities.

4. Choose learning over seeking approval: A lot of people wants to seek approval from people all the time. If you have to be a person with a growth belief, you should prioritize learning over seeking approval. When you are more concerned about getting approval from other people than about learning new things, you are giving up your own potential to grow. Don't worry about what other people think about you, and instead focus on bettering yourself for your own benefit.

5. Focus on the process instead of the end result: People who have a growth belief are often very in tune with their intelligence and willingness to learn. They understand that, any growth is going to be a process and therefore, make their own goals to help them reach the end of the process. It is important to enjoy the learning process so you are able to get the most out of it, and be open to the process continuing beyond the expected time frame. One of the most important things about the process of learning is the unexpected lessons that you may pick up along the way.

6. Cultivate a sense of purpose: People with a growth belief are able to look at long-term goals and have a larger sense of purpose for their lives. Keep the end goal in mind and always look at a bigger picture. Ask yourself on a regular basis what is the purpose of the work that you are doing. Are you doing it because you enjoy it, or is it part of a bigger goal? Always work with a purpose so you have the motivation to keep working.

7. Choose learning well over learning fast: This goes back to focusing on the process of learning instead of the end result. Learning isn't something that you can rush. You have to go through some mistakes in order to truly find success, and none of that will come easy or quickly.

8. Reward effort and actions, not traits: Let other people know when they are doing something creative or especially smart rather than just telling them that they are smart in general. This helps people strive to continue to do smart things rather than make them feel like they have already accomplished the end goal of being smart.

9. Learn to give and receive constructive criticism: Think of criticism as a way to learn. If you have an area of weakness and someone is able to point that out to you, think of it as a gift that makes you aware of your faults so you can focus on them to improve. It is important not to take constructive criticism personally. Often, people are trying to help and are therefore, doing you a favour rather than trying to cut you down. If you want to enhance your growth belief, learn to give and receive constructive criticism and think of criticism as a way to learn.

10. Need for improvement does not mean failure: Just because you need to improve in one area does not mean you have failed. It means that you are on the right track. You're just not quite there yet but definitely, somehow, someday you will get there.

11. Reflect on your learning every day: Make sure to absorb everything you learn throughout the day, whether this means writing down the main points at the end of the day or doing a little bit more research on a topic that held your interest the most that day. Don't let your lessons from the day just float away. Write it down in a bullet journal or make some other form of permanent record. At a minimum time, sit with the idea of what you learnt for a while and allow all the lessons to sink in.

12. Learn from the mistakes of others: You don't always want to compare yourself to other people, but it is important to see that other people have the same weaknesses as you are. When you see someone make a mistake and recognize how it should have been done correctly, keep that in mind for the future when you are in their situation. You can even put yourself in their shoes for the moment and pretend that it was you making the mistake, and try to learn from it first-hand.

13. Think of learning as "brain training": The more you learn, the more you are training your brain to act a certain way and make various connections. You want to train your brain as best as you can, which equates to learning throughout life. Your brain will have to be trained and retrained as the world evolves and things change, so it is vital to be open to the idea of manipulating your brain to keep up with current trends.

14. Cultivate perseverance: You want to have a passion for what you are doing so you can have the perseverance to see it through. Having a deep interest in your work is one of the most important things to keep you believing in yourself and motivated each day and to keep you wanting to be successful in your field. In order to accomplish your long-term goals, you have to have the perseverance to keep you inspired and on track. The only way you get motivated from the inside is when you have your self-belief in view.

15. Never stop learning: Set a new goal for every one you accomplish. You will never completely finish learning. Just because you have finished one class or one project does not mean that you should abandon the subject. Growth-minded people are able to continue to create new goals so they stay motivated and interested in the subjects that they choose to study or field they choose to specialize. Learning is never finished, as there is always another goal to reach or more research to be done. No wonder this famous quote says, ***"Never stop learning because life never stops teaching."***

16. Remember that it takes time to learn: Nothing worth doing comes quickly and easily. You have to be realistic about the time it will take for you to learn the information that you are interested in to the point of your satisfaction. It may take several different methods of learning or several times of applying a new technique until it really sticks and you are able to master it. Additionally, because things are constantly changing, this means that the learning process may never truly be over.

Make A Decision To Grow

In order to develop a growth belief, you have to be willing and committed to changing your beliefs about what you are able to do. You cannot stay wrapped up in the idea that you were born with all of your talents and abilities, and have no room to grow. You also have to take the appropriate actions to learn and stay motivated by looking at the bigger picture of why you have chosen to study what you have, and how it will benefit you in the long run. By figuring out the best ways that you learn, you can combine these learning tactics to provide yourself with the most lasting and effective lessons to improve upon your gift and serve it to the world.

Chapter Three

The Day My Life Changed

"In the middle of difficulties, lies opportunities" – Albert Einstein

Being the last born of six children to a first wife in a polygamous marriage was really challenging to me. I had everything in my environment to make me behave like the culture of our family set up and be limited by those principles. When I lost my dad in the year 2010, my life changed from luxury to suffering. I had never ever faced any difficult in my life until my father's sudden death. He was the centre of my living, because I had everything I wanted. Soon after my father was buried, my father's family started with maltreatments and denying us of our father's properties. It was rather unfortunate for me and my senior brother as we were very young to know and fight for what belongs to us. My brother and I are the last two kids of my mother. Unfortunately, the men to fight for the family were very young. Our elderly sisters couldn't stand the family. We went into years of difficulties as my life became miserable and disturbed. My education was under threat, my dreams and ambitions were fading away. I lost hope, not only did I lose hope but, the believe that things will get better as I lost everything and had to start from scratch. The maltreatment grew so hard that, we had to be deprived of access to electricity, water and other basic needs by my father's family. But through this, I discovered that, **"most of our obstacles would melt, if instead of crawling before them, we should make up our minds to walk boldly through them with the believe that we will overcome."**

His siblings were in a struggle for his properties, even siblings that were in grudges with him before he died claimed benefits from his properties. We had no one on our side but God. We were so different from our father's family; our beliefs, ways of doing things, and lifestyles were different. Perhaps this created a deep gap between our father's family and us.

Anyone Can Do It

"Impossible is just a big word thrown around by small men who find it easier to live in the world they've been given than to explore the power they have to change it. Impossible is not a fact. It's an opinion. Impossible is not a declaration. It's a dare. Impossible is potential. Impossible is temporary. Impossible is nothing." – Muhammad Ali
One morning, I woke up and started thinking; my life right now is shaking, my destiny and my ambitions are falling off my grasps. I have to do something. I am young but I don't want to be in my 50's and 60's to be successful or achieve all I have dreamt of. I want to be successful in my mid 20's and 30's and achieve all I want. Not that

I want too much too fast, no! That's what I believe in according to my life goals. Then I realized, if I sit down and lament over what I have lost and never do anything on my own, I would waste my life. Because the success I was enjoying was from my father not what I have built on my own. I have to do something on my own so others will benefit from that too. I also realized that, my father's life was an example for me to follow. Therefore, I began to hustle by looking for jobs to make ends meet. I remember going to the bus station to be a *'mate'*.

I walked around the market to carry loads for people so I could make money. I went hunting for birds and sold them at the market, I went gathering pure water sachet bags to sell as well as collecting scrubs (aluminium) to sell. I did everything I could do to get money for myself because I couldn't depend on anybody for lunch or dinner not even to think of breakfast. I had completed Junior High School at that moment. Because of the riots and chaos at home, I couldn't further my education into high school the same year. My father's family were making money from selling and renting my father's properties whiles we went hungry and suffering. I don't know for my step siblings but I believe they also faced some kind of difficulties but ours I think was worse.

I went on to work at a construction site and manufacturing companies. I was working as a labourer after some companies had refused to give me employment for being a minor. Not forgetting working as a labourer, helping with the construction of my church auditorium (True Light Worship Centre). I left the family and went to sleep in our uncompleted church auditorium as living in the family house became more unbearable. I did most jobs that could make me survive. I trusted the process so well and was never concerned with the pain as my focus was with the gain in the future.

I Made A Decision

"The best thing I ever did was to believe in myself"
One Wednesday morning after morning devotion, I was lying on the floor in the church auditorium, I begun to think about everything that was happening to me at the moment, I questioned my faith and believe in God. Friends were mocking at me, questioning my church going, sacrifice and dedication to church activities. Most of my friends went into fraud, they were making money. They rented big apartments and bought cars. They persuaded me to join them as I was very good with computers, fast communicator with a better communication skills and could be an important asset to them, but I refused. I was groaning in frustration. My spiritual father, Prophet James Owusu always gave me a prophecy that, I will go back to school and I am going to get a scholarship. He kept on saying these prophetic words to me for months. Her sister Lady Pastor Gladys also gave me a prophecy that God is giving me a helper soon.

I didn't believe them as none was manifesting. Later that year we had our annual mega convention and I said to God *"if by the end of the program, nothing happens to my life I will not come to church again and will go and join my friends to fraud."* From Monday to Friday nothing happened to me. Sunday morning I said to God before going to church, *"God today is my last day if you are going to be silent up there and watch people mock you that's up to you"*. Apostle Dr. Paul Oko Hackman was ministering that faithful day. I was sitting on the altar in the midst of the instrumentalist and when he was about to end his ministration, the *"injury time"* I call it. The Apostle of God called me and ministered unto me. He gave me a prophetic word saying, **"You're the light of your family and there is so much greatness in you."** He hugged me strongly that I felt the embracement of my biological father and he gave me a 100% scholarship for my Senior High School education. God bless him so much—not only did he sponsor me but I found another father to lean on. He anointed me and prayed for me immensely. **"The day I thought of giving up was the day my breakthrough was waiting for me."**

At often times a lot of people give up at the brink of their breakthroughs. They invest so much of their efforts and resources and when they get to an inch of receiving and enjoying their hard work efforts they give up and try something else. I could have missed that service and never experience that breakthrough in my life and blame God for not being faithful to me and see my spiritual father as a false prophet. I strongly believe that most of the prophecies we receive and never see it manifest is because we give up working on them. We sit down and think everything would manifest on a silver platter.

How I See Self-belief

"The greatest gift you'll ever receive is the gift of loving and believing in yourself. Guard this gift with your life. It is the only thing that will ever be truly yours." – Tiffany Loren Rowe

I see belief **as the mechanism that regulates what we accomplish in life.** If we look at a person who is settling for mediocrity, he believes he is worth little, so he settles for little and he receives little.

He does not believe he can do great things, so he does not. Most at times, belief endues us to do what others consider impossible. The act of believing is the starting force, the generating power that leads to greater achievement in life. Trusting yourself, having faith, possessing confidence are means of having self-belief. There are other contributing factors to the belief in one's self which includes physical and social presence, self-reliance and independence. Most of our actions, body language and speech reflect our level of confidence.

In essence, people who lack a solid self-belief relate to themselves more negatively, while people with self-belief are more positive about themselves and have higher self-esteem. A lot of people suffer with lack of self-belief at one point in their life. Recognizing that your self-belief could be a boost is equivalent to admitting that something could improve in your life. When your self-belief increases, you begin to grow and improve in unexpected ways. Very often, you may even notice that, you have been able to attract more positive and supportive people as well.

Chapter Four

Unleash Your Potential

"Potential is everything that is yet unused and is still within you"
– Dr. Myles Munroe

In other words, your potential is what you could do, but you've not done yet. If you have done something in the past never be impressed about it. It is no longer your potential. The cemetery today is a habitat of great potentials and in fact, if it could be mined like gold, the miner would be the wealthiest man on earth. The cemetery consist of great potentials that was never initiated, discovered or perhaps utilized. It consist of books that were not written, ideas that were not executed, philosophies that were not published. Inventions that were never invented, songs that were never written, visions that were never manifested, sermons that were never preached and so on and so forth. Millions of people have died without realizing their potentials which is the greatest inner abilities they possessed. They could have done great things with their potentials, but either ways—they failed to unleash their potentials and died to the grave with their inert abilities robbing the world of their divine gift.

Trapped In Every Creature Is An Uncommon Potential

"Your potential is limitless like the heavens" – Richmond George Ahornor

The greatest trap of moving ahead and improving upon your potentials is being excited about what you've done. You should never allow what you've done to stop you from doing what you can. If you stay excited to whatever you have done in the past and never learn to explore your capabilities in order to do more in the future you would never progress in life.

"Everyone has inside of him a piece of good news. The good news is that you don't yet realize how great you can be! How much you can accomplish and what your potential is." – Anne Frank

If you knew that, anything you want in life, your mind has the power to get them. You'll be half way through to get what you want. When you believe in your potential and unleash them, you will accomplish in few months what will take the average person who has not unleashed his potential several years to accomplish. You have a potential which is trapped inside you. Albert Einstein adds ***"Everybody is a genius. But if you judge a fish by its ability to climb a tree, it will live its whole life believing that it is stupid."*** Never allow yourself to think you're stupid or useless because you cannot do a particular thing. There is more to what you couldn't do. You can figure out, what potential is trapped within you.

Believe In Your Potential

"Your willingness to create a new dream or vision for your life is a statement of belief in your own potential." – David McNally

We all know that whatever you believe in works for you, maybe you don't but if you can start believing in something, that thing will come and be part of you and will always work for you. You cannot unleash and live to your full potential if you do not believe in it. There will be no obstacles you cannot overcome, a problem you cannot solve, a goal you cannot attain, a dream you can never manifest when you begin to believe in the potential of your amazing self. It's so common these days to get caught up in negative self-talk. It's also human nature to take your potential for granted and even doubt yourself when times are tough in life—in essence, being able to actively and consistently believe in your potential is very important.

To believe in yourself, you must first have knowledge about your potential—whatever you were born to do, you were built with. Looking at recent trends and developments in the world today, we are tamed to do what everybody is doing, the trends, what society accepts and not what we are destined for. Our friends, teachers, parents, as well as people close to us have looked down upon our potential and thought it to be useless. I remember before completing junior high school, I was making a decision for my course of study in senior high school. One of my sisters didn't want me to offer Visual Arts. That was my potential, my passion and I believed so much in it but I was discouraged and told not to opt for it. The reason being, Visual Arts students are rascals, they don't have a better future, they are not serious students and they don't get better jobs after school which they end up as sign writers and earn a little.

This was the misconception people had with the Visual Arts course. During our time, 1/10 parents will encourage or agree with their wards to offer visual arts. However, I ended up choosing General Arts as my course of study and luckily for me when my mum and I got to the school I was placed, the admission officers told my mum there's no vacancy for General Arts and the only classes available for me are, Visual Arts, Science and Agric Science. I smiled and called my spiritual father and told him about the situation. He asked me *"Son, what do you want to do?"* I said *"Visual Arts"* He replied *"Go for it son, that's part of your greatness."* Filled with so much strength I did not hesitate to choose Visual Arts.

I would boldly say without doubt, that I was an exceptional visual arts student and I did not exhibit all the misconceptions about visual arts students which earned me leadership positions in the SRC, Editorial Board & PENSA after loosing the race for school prefect. After completion of my Senior High School education, I became a successful creative designer in the creative industry without struggle but with believe and passion. My designs are widely accepted by great people. When someone thinks design, print or branding, the person thinks of me. It has given me the opportunity to go to places and met great people I would never have met if I gave up on it, because I believed in my potential as a creative person and my love for arts.

I acknowledged the fact that I am responsible for my life. Therefore, it is my sole responsibility to choose what I want to become. I can never be a pilot, a doctor or a lawyer because I don't want to and through creativity and inspiring people I would become great.

Indeed, today by having the believe in myself and potential, I am currently furthering my education at the university, by myself and for myself, whiles I have other projects and businesses I am working on. I am now a strong pillar for my family and anyone close to me as I strive to be an asset to my generation—I am obsessed by the progress I have been able to make within 4 years. I know my sister will be ashamed of preventing me from offering Visual Arts but today she is a benefactor and enjoying my creative skills and she now believes in me and my potential so much. The dreams and potential of people have been shut and destroyed because of what society thought about a career or a job. If you're a parent, do not decide the potential of your child. Discover your child's potential, believe in it and support him or her to be the best at it. I see no reason why a medical doctor will be worried because people with legal issues are looking for the lawyer. Be in your lane and believe in it. Your potential can never be something you decide, it's something you discover.

Thomas Edison

As a young boy, Thomas Edison's teachers told him he was *"too stupid to learn anything."* He did not have much more success in the workplace as he was fired from his first two jobs for not being productive. Even as an inventor, reports claim that Edison made 1,000 unsuccessful attempts at inventing the light bulb. Happily for night owls across the globe, attempt 1,001 worked out differently.

Albert Einstein

Today the word *"Einstein"* is synonymous with genius, but young Albert didn't speak fluently until he was 9 years old, causing teachers to think he was slow. He was expelled from school for his rebellious nature and was refused admission to the Zurich Polytechnic School. He went on to revolutionize science's understanding of the world, taking physics beyond its Newtonian view by developing the theory of General Relativity. He won the Nobel Prize, with his research leading the U.S. to build an atomic bomb, and influenced all aspects of culture, from religion, to art, to late-night television.

These two great men believed in their potential and the difference they could make with it and ended serving the world with their uncommon potential. Because they believed so much in their inherent ability and what they carry within they did not allow what their teacher told them to make an impact in their becoming. Others thought they were dumb and would be useless but in essence, no one saw they could even make history and will be forever celebrated but they fought every obstacle with belief and they reached the top.

Be The Best At What You Do

"If a man is called to be a street sweeper he should sweep streets even as a Michelangelo painted, or Beethoven composed music or Shakespeare wrote poetry. He should sweep streets so well that all the hosts of heaven and earth will pause to say, "Here lived a great street sweeper who did his job well." – Martin Luther King Jr.

To be the best, you will have to do what you do well. Never switch into a different career because of trends. If you're a sales man; be the best at it. If you're a cobbler, be unique among cobblers and be the best. No matter what you may be doing for a living be the best at it. One of the qualities of top people is that, at a certain point in their careers, they decided to **"Commit to Excellence."** They decided to be the best at what they do. They decided to pay any price, make any sacrifice, and invest any amount of time necessary to become very good in their chosen fields. Two years ago, I happened to listen to the Dean of Motivation—Earl Nightingale, I heard a voice that changed everything about my approach to what I do. He said ***"If you will spend one extra hour each day studying your chosen field, you will be a national expert in that field in five years or less."*** If you focus at least half hour study of your field of endeavour to be the best at what you do for five consecutive years you not only transform yourself to be the best at what you do but you transform the world around you. If it will cost you to learn, go to conferences and seminars, research on trends and changes in your field of specialty, do it. Improve on your skills, that's your call of duty to sell to the world.

No skill or potential, work or service is greater than the other. Everything you do, there's a demand for it. If you can believe in what you do and see that as your life and work hard to be fulfilled and not content but improve upon yourself then you can become great. It is not always about how much you make from what you do. If you are the best at it, that alone creates a value for you and you get to triple the leverage you make. Value what you do. Before someone respects your work, he or she has to see the respect you give it yourself. Because it is what you can do that will make you great. Therefore, there's a need to invest in it. Sometimes it's even not about connections or money, it's the willingness to outwork and out learn everyone when it comes to your business or career.

Create Specific & Definite Goals

Tom Hopkins says, "Goals are the fuel in the furnace of achievement." Your goals are the greatest possession you can have to achieve all you want; they give you a sense of meaning and purpose. Your purpose and sense of meaning lies in the goals you create for yourself. It serves as a directional map to your destiny. You only become happier and stronger when you see progress in your life as you move towards the attainment of your goals. You become more confident and competent in your potential and abilities.

Your belief in yourself increases by the step you take towards your goals and creates the confidence that you can even achieve bigger goals in the future. Your goals enable you to overcome any hindrance, and makes your future unlimited. You'll agree with me that; ***"A man without goal is like an arrow without a target, it shoots into any direction, and a man with a goal is like an arrow shot straight to its true target."*** Maybe you never knew, that anything you think about most of the time grows and increases in your life. If you are thinking, talking, and visualizing your goals, you tend to achieve far more than the average person, who usually thinks and talks about his or her problems most of the time.

Success Is Goals; Achieving Goals Makes You Successful

"Success is goals and all else is commentary" – Brian Tracy
Successful people think about their goals most of the time. As a result, they are continually moving toward their goals, and their goals are continually moving toward them. My spiritual father, Prophet James Owusu in one of his sermons on success defined it as ***"the progressive achievement of your goals."*** The dictionary also

defined success as *"the accomplishment of an aim or purpose."* These definitions clearly identifies that, to be able to measure your success there is a need to achieve a set goal, aim or purpose. To count your success you have to achieve a goal or aim. Success is not making a lot of money; it's not about having a big house or a car, success is not having a lot of people around you. Success is the completion and the fulfilment of the original intent or purpose for your existence or why a thing was made.

If a mother wants to put her child to sleep by 6pm and she is able to do that by 6pm, she is successful. In a situation where you want to increase your earnings to $10,000 by the end of the year and you are able to get it or more, then you're successful. For every goal you set and achieve counts the success you make for yourself. A famous Greek philosopher, Aristotle said *"man is a teleological organism."* The word *"teleos"* in Greek means *"goals."* That is to say, man is automatically *goal oriented.* Set your goals high and do something every day to move forward to achieving them.

Why We Don't Set Goals

"People are not lazy. They simply have impotent goals—that is, goals that do not inspire them." – Tony Robbins

After reading books on goal setting, I wanted to find out why goal setting is difficult for people to do which requires no effort and yet people fail to set goals including myself. Whenever I want to know someone I mostly ask *"what are your life goals"* and they end up telling me their dreams or wishes and yet classify them as goals. Until a desire, dream, wish or target is clearly written and specified, they are not goals. I discovered that, a lot of us do not recognize the importance of goal setting. We were brought up or grew up in a family or society where people are not clear and committed to their goal or perhaps have none at all and are only living by dreams or wishes. We grow up into adulthood without realizing our ability to set and achieve goals. However, others do not know how to set goals. Sadly, people think they already have goals when in reality, they only have series of wishes and dreams such as *"Be rich", "Have a lovely family", or "Be famous"*. But the hard truth is, these are not goals—they are all fantasies that are mostly common to everyone.

A goal **"is clear, written and specific"**—you can easily describe to someone, measure it, or know if achieved or not. The fear of failure is another discovery which cannot be exempted. If you fear to fail so you don't set goals, you end up going through life functioning at far lower level than what is truly possible for you. Some have the thought that friends or family will mock or criticize them. To avoid being ridiculed or mocked you have to keep your goals to yourself and prove by results and achievements.

I remember having a chat on Facebook with one of my networking partners in US. It was around the ending of December that year and was asking him of his 'New Year Resolutions', and he said *"I try not to commit myself totally to any resolution that way I don't set myself up for disappointment or failure."* Although he went on to say *"I do not mean to sound like I don't have ambitions or goals, because I do."* He may be driving his life on goals without time, and not written as well, why? Because of failure or disappointment. He thinks when he sets them unaccomplished, it will torment him. He is running away from failing. He does not believe in himself that whatever goal or resolutions that he will set he will surely accomplish them. That is how most of us are living our lives right now. We fear to rise and set goals, we fear to confront our fears and make things work for us.

Goals Makes Life Simple

"Create a goal—it will increase your confidence, develop your competence and establish your level of motivation." – Richmond George Ahornor

If you're clear about what you want; you automatically understand what you have to do. Visualize arriving on the outskirts of Accra and I tell you to drive to my office in Dansoman. Unfortunately, there are no road signs and you have no map of the city. In fact, all I gave you was just a general description of my office and that becomes your goal. Now how long do you think it would take you to find my office in a city without a road map or without road signs? Perhaps the rest of your life or even not at all. If you ever did find my office, it would be very much a matter of difficult adventure with a lot of agonies. And sadly enough, this is the way we live our lives.

Starting life without goals and plans is like traveling through an unmapped and uncharted world with no road signs. We assume we are on course and after 10 or 20 years of work will go past and we're still broke, unhappy in our jobs, dissatisfied with our marriage and making little or no progress. And yet, we get home every night to watch television, wishing and hoping that things would get better. But they seldom do. The goals you set makes your future secured and unlimited.

Achieving Goals Brings Happiness

"Your goals are one of the greatest possessions you can have to achieve all you want; they give you a sense of meaning and purpose."
– Richmond George Ahornor

I find desire as the greatest driving force to the attainment of your goals. To achieve your goals and enjoy happiness you need to have a driving tool that is **relentless desire**. You have to develop a powerful burning desire. It is only when your desire becomes strong enough that you will have the energy and the internal drive to overcome all the obstacles that will arise on your path. The good news is that almost anything that you want long enough and hard enough, you can ultimately achieve.

In one of the teachings of Aristotle, he concludes that, the ultimate purpose of all human action is the achievement of personal happiness. Whatever you do, he said, **"it is aimed at increasing your happiness in some way. You may or may not be successful in achieving happiness, but your happiness is always your ultimate aim (goal)."**

After setting your goals, working towards its attainment daily and achieving them brings happiness in your life. Goal setting is so powerful that the very act of thinking about your goals make you happy, even before you take the first step toward achieving them. Anytime you hit and miss a goal you have set; don't give up nor change it—try again. Even look at your life right now and remember certain little things you planned to do in the past and you were able to do them. Look at the joy it brought to you. How much more than your greatest achievement you have been desiring all your life. There is no greater guarantee of a long, happy, healthy and prosperous life than for you to be continually working on being, having and achieving more and more of the things you really want.

How To Set Goals

According to Brian Tracy, here is his simple seven-step formula for setting and achieving goals, which has helped me in the past three years;

First, decide exactly what you want in each area of your life, especially in your financial life. Most people never do this.

Second, write down your goals clearly and specifically. Something amazing happens between your head and your hand when you put your goals in writing.

Third, set a deadline for each goal. Set sub-deadlines if a goal is big enough. Give yourself a target to aim at.

Fourth, make a list of everything you can think of that you will have to do to achieve each goal. As you think of new ideas, add them to your list until it is complete.

Fifth, organize your list into a plan of action. Determine what you are going to do first and what you will do later. Decide what is more important and what is less important.

Sixth, take action on your plan immediately. It is amazing how many splendid goals and plans are never realized because of procrastination and delay.

Seventh, most importantly, do something every day that moves you at least one step closer to your most important goal. This commitment to daily action will make you a big success in anything you decide to accomplish.

Chapter Five

The Essence of Time

"You can always make more money; but you cannot make more time" – Richmond George Ahornor

To believe in yourself and be successful at anything you try, you must be able to control and manage your time well. Like any other skill, time management is a skill and it can be learned—no matter how you have been disorganized in the past, or wasted some years and tend to be a procrastinator; you can get back on truck and make the rest of the years ahead a special one. Irrespective of these sudden events, if you decide in your mind and believe in yourself, you can become one of the most effective and efficient productive people in whatever you intend to do. I have seen most people who discovered the importance of time and have been able to be transformed from confusion to clarity and from frustration to focus, so why can't you also do it? It doesn't take a decade to be happy or rebuild a better side of life. There is no doubt that, to believe in yourself, achieving your ambitions and becoming great in life you have to be time conscious. ***Undoubtedly, time is a resource.***

You will agree with me that there are only two events in your life; thus birth and death, and what happens between these two events is very important that you should make use of it. Whatever that happens between these two events is limited and controlled by time. We have no idea what the distance between birth and death is going to be. Time is like a flowing river, the moment it passes, it doesn't come back and when you fetch a portion you cannot fetch the same portion again. ***"It is useless to desire more time if you are already wasting what little you have". – James Allen***

Time is all we have this moment, right now and it is only one thing in our lives that we will never be able to re-acquire once it's gone. It's not money or material things, it's a valuable resource thus time and in such a unique idea when utilized and managed correctly, it contains one of the ingredients to success, happiness, growth, prosperity and all the things we want. But, when neglected, it leaves us with very little. We shouldn't forget the fact that we are living minutes, we will never get back and breathing air, we will never breathe back. ***"A great amount of time lost, to me is a time not started for anything; do something now." – Rev. Alexander Agyapong***
A lot of people are wasting their time on things that doesn't need to be done and later desire more time to get what needs to be done which they regret. What else can we do now as it seems to be our opportunity to embrace this gift and to seize a moment to make every minute count than to let it slip away? When people tell me

they would do anything for a little more time; I find it ironic as they desire more time and yet waste the time they already have. ***"Time is life's greatest leveller" says Robin Sharma.*** There is no doubt that everyone has 24 hours in a day, and what differentiates people who build great lives and are very successful from the non-successful people is how they use these hours. Most of us live as if, we have an unlimited amount of time to do all the things we know we must do to live a full and happy life. As novelist Paul Bowles once wrote:

"Because we don't know when we will die, we get to think of life as an inexhaustible well. Yet everything happens only a certain number of times, and a very small number, really. How many more times will you remember a certain afternoon of your childhood, some afternoon that's so deeply a part of your being that you can't even conceive of your life without it? Perhaps four or five times more. Perhaps not even that. How many more times will you watch the full moon rise? Perhaps twenty. And yet it all seems limitless."

Invest Your Time

Never forget to dedicate yourself to managing your time more effectively. Develop a sense of awareness about the importance of your time. Don't allow people to waste this most precious moment and invest it only in the activities that truly counts according to your goals and purpose in life. There is no moment more important than right now, not tomorrow, a week, a month or a year. It is sad that we are made to believe that when we suffer today, we are going to enjoy tomorrow. We have the mentality that the future is going to mean more than the present. When we are uncomfortable, unhappy or living a low life now, we save the best in life for some other time which is the future but the hard truth is—we don't get any younger, yes and we should be working hard. It is true that success comes from hard work, dedication, commitment, discipline but it is also important to allocate our precious time to work on ourselves and the things that make us feel like today is so powerful. That right now is so amazing and you don't want it to end. When you believe in yourself and become who you want to become, no one can take that from you unless yourself. There is no special requirement. You too can become great and make good use of your time. You are the only one who can allow or deny yourself to accomplish all you want, you are the gate keeper, you have your foot on the gas clutch.

It has become so easy to point out to others, to point to your environment and blame things on anything at your disposal. You are where you are because you have decided to be and that is okay to you. If you want change then you have to manufacture change. There is no time to waste, you have to do that now. Create a plan and move, go and transform, step out of your head into the real world realizing how lucky you are to be in an era where we have access to all the information we can dream of, technology that enables growth and freedom to pursue any career path that seems appealing.

Procrastination Doesn't Exist

"Tomorrow begins today" – Rev. Alexander Agyapong

I remember speaking at a youth gathering in one of the churches in Accra and after delivering my message, I gave the audience the opportunity to ask me questions about what troubles them, what habit they want to stop. To my surprise, there were a lot of questions and I took time to answer them with practical illustrations. But there is one that I would like to refer here. A young lady asked me, *"Please, I'm always a victim of procrastination how can I stop that?"* I started smiling and said to her, *"My dear, I personally believe, there is no such thing as procrastination; it does not exist. It's a matter of priorities."* From the expression on their faces they were confused and I explained. *"If I told you to meet me at Kempiski Hotel for GH¢10,000.00 tomorrow at 8am, where would you be?* She quickly replied *"I'd be right there at 7:45am."* And everyone burst into laughter.

This is a clear indication that procrastination does not exist, it's a matter of priorities. She would ignore everything she has to do in the morning and meet me at the mall even before 8am; why? Because the money is important to her and therefore her meeting with me is her outmost priority and need. She wouldn't procrastinate it for anything. Everything else should wait. Then I concluded by saying, *"So now tell me where the hell is procrastination?"* It is without doubt that by now there shouldn't be anything like procrastination in your life. You must set your priorities right and have time for things that are important to you. If they are not important to you, they are done or attended later. Time is a valuable resource and therefore you cannot afford to waste it doing the things that are not important to you or wouldn't move you towards your aim or goals in life.

You have to move from a ***"tomorrow person to a right now person."*** Everything that is going to benefit your life and improve your life and boost your confidence has to be done immediately and daily. You don't have to push it to another day. I need you at this point to set your priorities right. Even if you tell me you're going to do something today, you have the whole day, there shouldn't be any tomorrow or today but it should be right now and get going to improve your life and develop your confidence for a successful living. Look back at the things you could have accomplished but failed because you kept procrastinating them. You keep moving them to next minute, hour, day, week, month, and year. Stop saying I'd do that later and do it right now. You said you are going to build a house, go to school, start a business, write a book or start that career, but so far as it is not executed. It is a dream and not a goal not to talk of becoming a reality.

"Anything you want to do or start tomorrow, you can start now."
– Rev. Alexander Agyapong

If you want to go farther in life, you have to delete procrastination from your dictionary. Anytime something you have to do drops in mind just do it immediately. Time flies and before you realize it's a decade and you have not even attained what you set to do and later regret for wasting those precious years. Time they say is money and those who manage and make good use of it become wealthy.

Chapter Six

The Top Five Questions

"Plain question and plain answer make the shortest road out of most perplexities." – Mark Twain

I know you would be wondering what top five questions I am going to talk about. According to Dr. Myles Munroe, every human being living on earth is motivated by these five questions and these questions control the universe, they control individuals, countries and leaders. These five questions are so important that they control the entire world. Everything that every human does on this earth is motivated by these five questions. Before you can believe in yourself and make your belief give you confidence, motivation and reason for your life, you need to answer these five questions about yourself. It is very important but most of us have missed these questions and living our lives anyhow and thereby settling for less than we deserve.

"To live is to choose. But to choose well, you must know who you are and what you stand for, where you want to go and why you want to get there." – Kofi Annan

I personally believe that what we were created to do more than we are doing right now. According to the Brain Myth, we have not used more than 15% of our potential on earth and settle for less not exploring, grow old and die to be buried in an average grave. The life of Jesus Christ has answered all five questions and I will quote him in each question what he answered about himself and what we can learn and apply from Him.

Who Am I? (Identity)

"When you know who you are, you put zero weight into anyone's opinions." – Garry Vaynerchuk

This is a difficult question to answer. Most people don't know who they are; they therefore seek the opinion of others on who they are, but truth be told, whenever you seek to find who you are from other people they will never make you more than who they are. You should know who you are before someone tells you who you should be because the discovery of who you are will make you fulfilled with what you have and where you are. Even celebrities find it difficult to answer this simple question.

I know it sounds simple but tricky. Who am I? Has to do with your identity, what you're made of. I asked a lady this question and she ended up telling me what she does; her profession. She said *"I'm an actress"* Though I was not asking her what she does, she ended up telling me, instead of telling me who she is. At often times, we misinterpret who we are with what we do and we end up forgetting who we are and die as someone else. This question is the first step to the discovery your true self. It goes a long way to give you the revelation of the essence of your person. The greatest man in history, Jesus Christ was asked this question and from the greatest book in the history of man—the Bible; Jesus answered this question 7 times of which I will take one and talk about in relation to the context above. Then Jesus spoke to them again, saying, ***"I am the light of the world. He who follows Me shall not walk in darkness, but have the light of life." - John 8:12***

I read this scripture with deep insight, although it was not the first time I have come across the text. As I re-visited, I felt I have to solidify my point on this subject with a reference and I grabbed a different insight all together. Jesus was asked who he was, I can't recall him telling the people that he was a carpenter nor the son of Mary & Joseph. He never said what he does. But he directly and clearly said who he is and what he is made up of. He never wasted his time to be someone else or live another life that will take him out of who he is.

This is the first question you must answer on your journey to greatness and believing in yourself of whoever you intend to be. ***"I am the light of the world…"*** A point blank answer. Although there were many predictions on who he was, he truly knew within him and did not consider any other opinion or predictions of who he was to be his true identity. There is a lot to learn from this scripture. If you know who you are, you become bold and confident. If you can identify yourself very well, you will accomplish in few months, what will take someone without self-identity to accomplish in five years.

Where Am I From? (Source)

"All our dreams can come through if we knew our source of greatness."
– Richmond George Ahornor

Where you are from, is talking about your source, not your ethnicity or race. It is not about whether you come from Africa, Asia, America or Australia. It is also not about you being black or white. It is your source that determines your strength and your ability. The source of something determines the strength and ability of that thing. I remember reading about the origin of human and I came across an article which said, **"man came from a monkey, a salamander that crept on the rock 6 million years ago and became a tadpole and became a frog which also became a monkey and also became a man".** Some really believe in that!

When you can find out where you came from, you can also find out your ability, your strength and potential. In the same vein when you're unable to find out where you come from; you can never know what you are made of, what your qualities are, as well as your abilities. The strength of something is determined by what it's made of—thus its source. Supposing there is a leather product, maybe a shoe or a sandals. The durability and flexibility of the product will not be determined by the one who designed it, but it will be determined by the source. The type of animal skin it was slew from.

Some don't believe they were created by God and if you happened to be one of them, that's fine; I don't have a problem with that—but here's the divine truth, God is the creator of the world and everything in it. It is written in the Old Testament in the book of Genesis 1:27 **"So God created man in His own image; in the image of God He created** *him; male and female He created them."*

Do not allow any philosophy or scientific research to deceive you of your source but I will encourage you to believe that you have a source and therefore your source is God—which makes you unlimited and powerful being. *"Yet for us there is [only] one God, the Father, Who is the Source of all things..." 1 Cori. 8:6 (AMPC)* You should keep that in mind and be able to believe in your source for strength and ability without limitation. Jesus Christ again on his existence on earth has always answered these five questions and he answered His source as well. In the book of John 8:42 *"Jesus said to them, "If God were really your Father, you would love me. I came from God and now I am here".*

There was a clear response of the source of Jesus Christ. He knew who he was and where he came from. Don't you think because He knew his source, He believed in Himself and what He could do? Probably, that gave Him some uncommon strength and ability to do an uncommon work. He knew He came from God Almighty, the All-powerful so therefore, whatever is in His source, is also in Him.

Therefore, if you believe you came from a monkey, an ape or whatever your source is, you behave according to it; that is why people always settle for less and blend in to what society has taught us to live by. And for those who believe they were created by God, fearfully (created with care) and wonderfully made, know that your source has the greatest power. Therefore, your creator is the most powerful in the world you exist in. Whatever power your creator has, He has instilled in you to do exploits and fulfil that potential you have. Don't seek your source from the opinion of others, never allow any lecturer, society, philosophy, friends or family to deny you of knowing your source.

Why Am I Here? (Purpose)

"You're not here by mistake." – Ben Marrow

There's a reason why everyone is here. It's not a mistake or a coincidence that you're here and is therefore, important to find out why. The average human being does not know why he/she is on planet earth. They have settled for less and blended into society. Wake up every morning going to a job they hate, working with people they don't like and getting paid less than what they are worth and dying too young from frustration because they don't know why they exist.

"The greatest tragedy in life is not death, its life without a purpose. To be alive and not know why". – Dr. Myles Munroe

Do you think you came to planet earth to work, pay bills, retire and die? There is a purpose for your existence and you have to discover it. Some of us are breathing oxygen, eating food, getting energy and do not know why we have it. To live for 60years and still not know why we are here? ***"Without a purpose life has no meaning, it has no sense of direction."*** Everyone wants to be successful. No one plans to fail tomorrow. Success is predictable, and therefore your success has been designed by God to be predictable. Failure is also predictable. Success is predictable so you can literally plan it. God designed everything to be successful. You will never see a bird who cannot fly naturally, a fish who cannot swim. It was designed by God to succeed for a specific purpose. There is more to your life and existence than what you are living for. You have to discover your purpose. The purpose you were created for lies in this question and if you can answer it, you will be half way through.

Again in the New Testament, the book of John 12:47 ***"If anyone hears my words and does not keep them, I do not judge him; for I did not come to judge the world but to save the world"***. This is a short passage but it answers a lot. Jesus keeping in mind his purpose on earth and working daily to fulfil His purpose; He said, even though people will hear His message and not keep them, He will not judge them. He will not be concerned about them, He will not lament over them. He will not cry over them, He will not force anyone to keep His words because His purpose on earth is not to be concerned about what people say about Him. Who they think He is and what He came to do on earth. His purpose does not allow Him to talk about those who do not keep His words, nor allow Him to talk ill about them.

I attest that, by being concerned whether the people kept his words or not, He is deviating from His purpose. He is forfeiting why he is on planet earth but because His purpose (to save the world) is known to Him and so clear in His mind each and every day, people's opinion and reaction was not enough grounds to discourage Him to give up on His purpose. If everyone would be willing to put their purpose in mind, in view, believing they can fulfil it and working conscious daily towards it and not be distracted by the opinions of others, they will really be successful. You have to understand that, the moment you stand in for your purpose; people will stand against you and try to talk you out of your purpose but you have to stand strong and fight for your purpose no matter what as Jesus did.

What Can I Do? (Potential)

"Potential is a priceless treasure, like gold. All of us have gold hidden within but we have to dig to get it out." – Joyce Meyer

No one knows your ability except your creator; that is why you should never allow anyone to judge you based on their measurement, their tests or perceptions about you. A lot of teachers has destroyed the hidden potentials of many children, looking down on them and telling them they are dumb just because of a test they failed in class. Never allow anyone to tell you what you can do or not do. The moment you discover what you can do, you expose your potential. The average human on earth have no idea about their ability and the extent to which they can go to utilize their full potential.

Many percentage of the human population will die and never achieve more than 12% of their ability. Jesus Christ coming on earth was not ignorant about what He can do. He had in mind His potential and never allowed the rating of the Jews nor the Pharisees to take him out of His potential.

41 Jesus was indignant. He reached out his hand and touched the man. "I am willing," he said. "Be clean!" 42 Immediately the leprosy left him and he was cleansed. (Mark 1:41- 42) How did he do that? Through potential, He has the power to heal and He performed many miracles. What you can do is your potential.

"...Then he got up and rebuked the winds and the waves, and it was completely calm. 27 The men were amazed and asked, "What kind of man is this? Even the winds and the waves obey him!" (Matthew 8:26-27)

Jesus spoke and expedited His ministry with authority. He always knew what He was doing and what He can do. You should never be ignorant about your potential (what you can do). You will be amazed at the things you can do if you believe in yourself. Don't waste your time trying to blend in and not discovering what you can do, but rather spend most of your time doing, building and developing yourself in that direction. Don't allow anyone to tell you what your potential is, you have to answer for yourself and show people what you can do. Now if you believe in God the Father, the Son and the Holy Spirit then this is for you. ***"Now to him who is able to do far more abundantly than all that we ask or think, according to the power at work within us". (Ephesians 3:20)***

If you believe in God as your creator, according to the power (potential) at work in you, there's nothing you cannot do if you believe you can. Meanwhile, wherever you also believe you came from, you should know that there's a great potential in you that the world needs to encounter before you die.

Where Am I Going? (Destiny)

"There's no greater discovery than seeing God as the author of our destiny." – Ravi Zacharias

This is probably the last question and it has to do with destiny. What is my destination? Everyone wants to know what their future holds. For me, I am so optimistic about my future. You'll agree with me that you weren't born just to go to school, get a job, pay bills and die. Where are you going in the next 10 to 30 years? Ask yourself. Some of us can't wait. We want too much too fast. We are all on earth with different gifts to fulfil an assignment; which is our destiny.

The destiny of Jesus Christ was long prophesied by Major Prophets in the Old Testament before He was born. When He came on earth He knew His destiny thus to save the world. He fulfilled His destiny believing He could and He did. The same God also spoke to Jeremiah. ***"Before I formed you in the womb I knew you; before you were born I sanctified you; I ordained you a prophet to the nations." (Jeremiah 1:5)***

The destiny of Jeremiah was revealed to him when he questioned himself on his destiny. Irrespective of who you are and where you are from or what you are made of; you should know you are on earth going somewhere and life is a journey not a 100m dash or race. Everyone has a different destiny or destination. You are supposed to fulfil yours where you are; that's why you are in Africa, America, Asia, Australia or Europe and it's not by a mistake that you find yourself being black or white… ignore the fact that you're white or black, in Africa or Europe. You're not where you are because of a mistake. It's for a reason and if you can carry this belief in your mind you will do greater works. Don't wish you were somewhere or like someone because your destiny has been designed to be the way you are and you can only fulfil it being you. Don't try to be someone in other not to miss your originally designed destiny programmed by God.

There was a man looking for money to dig for oil, he knowing California is said to be one of the oil hubs in America, he decided to sell his piece of land and go to California to mine for oil. After selling his piece of land, he moved to California, six months later he was riding on a horse and saw in the newspaper the land he sold for $30,000 has oil and the buyer has discovered it. And making about $1million from it. He fell off his horse and died of heart attack. After reading this story, my spiritual father's quote came in mind and it reads; ***"Do what you can, with what you have, where you are."*** *– Prophet James Owusu*

The greatness you seek is right where you are, inside you. You need to ask yourself and seek no answer from anyone but yourself which makes you responsible for the life you live on earth. If your destiny is not solving a problem in the world then you're not making the world enjoy your destiny and why you came on planet earth. Knowing where you are going must remind you of the legacy you want to leave on earth before you die.

Chapter Seven

Your
Association

"Life is in connection, not in isolation." – Prophet James Owusu

Most of life's success is never achieved alone. In your quest to succeed at what you do and make an impact in your generation, your association with people in a positive way or a negative way can never be undermined. How you relate to people is very important. A critical determinant of your success in life is based on your association with people. At every level of your life, you need a certain type of association that will help you achieve all you want. The level of association you have in a positive way will have an impact on your success rate at anything you attempt. One positive relationship with someone at the right moment can initiate a breakthrough in your life or business that will change your life. Inversely, the same relationship with someone can also initiate a problem or a setback in your life or business that will affect you for the rest of your life. One of the elements of using your self-belief to achieve great things will require you to recognize certain people and fix them in your circle to achieve great things. It will require you to surround yourself with not just anybody, but positive people that you believe can help you achieve what you want in life. To be successful and develop your self-belief you will need help from people which will require you to get the right association you flow with.

Personally, I think there are some universal categories of people whose help and contributions you will need in the journey of your life. These people may include; the people in and around your business or career, your family and friends and people within groups or organizations in your social circle. Your effective association with these people in a positive way is very important. You will need to strategically flow with each category of people. Brooks Robinson wrote **"Associate with those who help you believe in yourself."** Always remember that, at every virtual point you stand, someone is standing there either to help you or hinder you for your next level in life. Associate yourself with optimistic and happy people who have goals and moving forward in life, because their life in a certain way will have a reflection in your life. Notwithstanding, move away from negative, critical, complaining people and be a go-giver rather than a go-getter.

It is believed that, there are two creatures on the planet, if you continually tell them they are bad, they will take it in and believe it; dogs and humans. We have all seen dogs whose spirits have been broken. They walk around with their tails between their legs and their heads down. They get startled or scared very easily, and can react with fear aggression (barking or growling when they are frightened). The poor thing never seem to feel safe and secure. They have lost their wag, and it's sad to see.

People tend to react in similar ways when they are living with someone who puts them down on a regular basis or they are working for a company that manages by intimidation. There is very little joy to be found here, and one's sense of self-believe can easily be shattered. Most people in such places are unable to find the strength they need to battle the forces that are attacking them because they have simply run out of energy.

Keep The Right People
Zig Ziglar said, "If you want to fly with the eagles, you can't continue to scratch with the turkeys".

The eagle is the only bird that can fly at a high altitude and they don't flock like other birds. When an eagle sees a bird at a higher altitude then it is another eagle. It is really clear that the association you keep has a major impact in your life and therefore must be checked. Don't keep and move along with the wrong people and expect to have a positive outcome. Dr. David McClelland of Harvard University did many years of research into the qualities and characteristics of high achievers in our society. He found out that, the people with whom you habitually associate with, was more important in determining your chances of success or failure. You should never forget to strive in your endeavour to associate with the right category of people whom you admire, like, respect and want to be like someday.

There are basically three levels of relationships you must keep.

- People you're ahead of—whom you can teach them what you know as you teach, you learn more.
- People you're in the same level with—whom you can share some ideas with and learn more from them.
- People that are ahead of you, they can be mentors—this level of people will broaden your mind as you can learn a lot from them.

After you learn from people that are ahead of, you then reach out to people you're in the same level with. You share what you learn then reach out to people you're ahead of and teach them what you have learnt. This is like a chain of actions. In each level, **you learn.**

Will Rogers said, **"A man only learns by two things; one is reading and the other is association with smarter people."** Imagine, there is an average person, with an average mind and beliefs, achieving average goals and in few weeks he changes his level of association with optimistic, result-oriented, go-ahead people. Without doubt, his output level will change because of his association. He will become optimistic, result-oriented as well. There will be an influence from the people he associates with, they will broaden his thinking capacity and his level of belief.

There are countless number of things you can do that you are not doing because you lack the right kind of association which will influence you and push you to the top. Certain beliefs are dead in you because one way or the other your present association has killed that belief. If you keep wrong relationships and associate with wrong people who are not going your way, they will change your belief and your way of doing things. A person can be calm, gentle but few months in school and upon encountering certain level of association, he changes. There has been an impact made on his life from his association. The association you keep can either make you successful or unsuccessful. This is why almost every major change in your life will be associated with a change in the people you live or work with.

Disconnect The Wrong People

"Keep away from people who try to belittle your ambitions. Small people always do that, but the really great make you feel that you too can become great". – Mark Twain

In life, who you walk with, determines what works for you. If you keep negative associations, negative things will happen to your life and your beliefs will be affected. Negative associations can change important priorities. In the journey of life, there is always someone you meet—this person has an influence in the direction you go and the doors you open or close. You should not spend your time with people who are not going your direction, irrespective of how nice they may seem to be. Some people you meet in life, are really nice and you might want to be with them for the rest of your life but the hard truth is they are not going your way or they are going nowhere at all. Don't waste your time with them. If you can remember from chapter five; you can always make more money but you cannot make more time. Life is also like a flowing water or a river, you cannot touch the same water twice. It passes so swiftly and if it passes it never comes back.

"You will be the same person in five years except for the people you meet and the books you read." – Charles Jones

If you believe in yourself and that you can achieve great things in life and leave a mark in your generation, you can't afford to spend your precious time with people who are going nowhere. Your future ambitions and beliefs should prompt you and remind you all the time of the people you associate yourself with. You must set a certain level of standard on the friends you make and the association you keep and refuse to compromise.

From the famous book, the Bible in Amos 3:3, **"Can two walk together, except they be agreed?"** You can never be comfortable walking with people you don't have the same mindset with. Thereby, if you keep the wrong association you have to do the wrong thing and doing the wrong things will cost you. If you happened to disagree with something within an association you have and you feel it is not in line with your beliefs and future ambitions, never hesitate to disconnect yourself from it. It will never help you achieve anything. You would do very well to separate yourself from distractions and companies that may derail your destiny. Never be afraid to let go of bad relationships.

In the Bible, Abraham got to the point where he decided to do away with wrong company. Never mind, they can be family or friends, but anyone that blinds you from your divine purpose is a destiny destroyer. Until Abraham separated himself from Lot that God clarified his divine purpose. Genesis 13:14, **"And the Lord said unto Abram, after that Lot was separated from him, Lift up now thine eyes, and look from the place where thou art northward, and southward, and eastward, and westward.."**

When I got to know this, whenever I come into contact with people, from all walks of life, firstly I ask them who they are, their sense of significance and why they are on planet earth. Basically this questions seeks to expose who they truly are, their state of mind and their life goals, whether they have something meaningful in life to do. If you don't have any set goals or ambitions I will never be your friend. When you have nowhere going and you become part of me you will automatically influence my direction into nowhere with you. And if what you seek in life has no connection with what I seek to accomplish, I will never keep you. No matter how nice you may be.

"No association leaves you neutral. When you walk with vultures you will eat carcasses; when you walk with confused people you become confused." – Prophet El-Bernard Nelson

A lot of people end up with bad relationships and form useless acquaintances and regret making them but the good news is, it's okay if you made such associations especially if you're young and inexperienced but you should never continue to make them. Useless acquaintances will hold you back from realizing your potential and believing in yourself that you could do something worthwhile in life. No wonder Dr. Mensa Otabil said, *"Never let the negative words of people kill your hopes and dreams."*

Self-belief cannot exist within an aura of meanness. To find yourself and rebuild what has been taken from you, disconnecting yourself from a negative environment and association may be the only solution. Throughout my life, I have not known any other single factor that has more impact on what you become than your choice of association. The issue of association is an issue of decision. You have to be decisive about who you allow to influence your life, or you miss it completely.

Make Your Associations Healthy

"Do unto others as you would have them do unto you."

This rule is very clear, specific and famous. You have to treat the people you meet and around you with kindness, courtesy and compassion. To keep your associations healthy you have to treat people like they are the most important people in the world. I heard a quote which left me thinking and have already shared what I discovered on my social media handles. I got a depth of it and its really interesting; **"Some people are so poor, all they have is money"**... after depth thinking, I got to know that, success is more than just monetary gain, life is a journey and its really about the people (association) who are walking with you throughout the journey. Your relationships, family and being content with your current blessings which usually comes too late in life if your focus is solely on wealth acquisition.

We shouldn't ignore the fact that a healthy association makes us rich within the soul, where even money merely makes an image. I will personally attest that building your dreams together within and around the right association is better than being rich alone. Not forgetting that life is in connection not in isolation. What you believe in, your family, network or association in that specific order are your true net-worth, they are your value. There is no progress in an association or environment where negativity and awful behaviour are encouraged. Whenever possible, choose to surround yourself with people who are positive and purposeful. In all the days of your life, every way possible, strive to help other people by reducing their load and make an impact rather than an income to make their lives or business successful. This practice will build a great reservoir of positive feeling and results towards you and will forever come back to you for your personal success in the days of your life and your descendants.

Chapter Eight

Fear —
The Hidden Thief

"Too many of us are not living our dreams because we are living our fear." – Les Brown

Every single person in the world wakes up each day, in battle against fear. Irrespective of who you are, you cannot avoid it, and you will never escape it. But that isn't to say you cannot overcome it. Yes, you can overcome it. We always think first; *"what if"* this doesn't work out? We build our lives on *"what ifs"* because we fear that if we don't succeed at what we try, we become a failure. A lot of people have died and never achieved anything worth in life because of fear. ***"What if—is the language of fear and the language of fear, is the language of the devil."*** No promotion in life, unequivocally, has never been met with equal level of opposition. Most successful people, past or present, who have achieved great feat in their pursuit had once tasted failure or opposition. Yet they didn't cower but demonstrated unflinching tenacity to succeed. Successful people ignore the *"what if"* thoughts by their fixed belief. You should never be afraid to fear. Fear is really necessary for courage to exist. Dr. Myles Munroe defined courage as the capacity to stand in the face of fear and failure. We all have something we fear being it rejection, embarrassment, loneliness, illness, job loss, failure so on and so forth. It is okay to fear but it is not okay to allow fear to stop you from believing in yourself and reaching your greatness. In the New Testament, Peter said, **"Do not fear what they fear; do not be frightened."** (1 Peter 3:14 CSB) The fear of others should not be your fear too. If fear stopped someone it shouldn't stop you. Believe in yourself and intimidate your fear rather than letting it intimidate you.

Fear Will Cost You

We all the time want to play it safe and never show ourselves to the world or prove what we are capable of. We become slaves to fear and all the time feel powerless, inferior and ready to give up and allow people to control and hurt us because we refuse to speak up for ourselves. There has been situations where marriages fail because fear stops one or both spouses to open up, to communicate, be honest, vulnerable or sexy. Good people stand at the sidelines and never make their mark, businesses fail because fear stops them from change and innovation.

At this point, there is no doubt that fear is a great usurper of progress and self-belief. It's a pity, but true that this century is littered with great men and women who simply let fear drive their lives and never realize to work hard and condition their minds to tame fear so as to choose consciousness over the ease of running away from life. Fear has no power over you. You have power over it. In essence, it is only you and you alone who can activate and deactivate fear. Have you ever imagined how the fire fighter enter into the furnace to save people? How the fishermen still go fishing even though they know the dangers of the storm? Maybe we don't believe in ourselves enough that we can make the choice to be more confident than fearful. When we pursue self-belief in everything we do, we discover our destiny and through fear we look at our demise.

It Will Stop You If You Let It

"Fear doesn't exist anywhere except in the mind." – Dale Carnegie

My neighbour was ejected by her landlord and she has a dog. Unfortunately for the dog, he was left in the house after the ejection and the gate was locked that nobody could bring him out. Several days went by and the dog was hungry, the dog broke his cage and seeking freedom to get something to eat. It scrolled through the house the whole day and nothing was in the house to feed on. So the dog decided to come out of the house so it could find something to eat. The dog managed to climb the wall since the height between the ground and the top of the wall in the house was not much because of a heaped sand near the wall. After climbing to the top of the wall, the dog needs to jump outside the house to get food and water to survive after starvation.

All this while I have been observing the dog and I could not tell why I was so interested in the situation of the dog. So I watched closely. It will be walking on top of the wall fearing to jump outside as the height between the ground outside to the top of the wall, where it was standing was a bit high and scary to the dog. It stood for hours looking for solutions by going left and right to see if it can find a safer place to jump but it found none. From the beginning, I stood smiling whiles watching. Due to fear that it could break the leg, the dog went back inside the house. The next day it came to the top of the wall. You could see the desire to jump outside the house to get food. The dog had freedom to flee from starvation but it refused. Why? Because it feared the depth of the floor from the wall. The dog was much concerned with the pain than the gain. This event by the dog was repeated for three days and never took the risk to flee from starvation and enjoy freedom. I agree with Brendon Burchard when he said ***"The solution to your fear lies in the middle of your action."*** If you never take action against your fear, you will never come out of it.

The dog never took one not because it didn't have one but because it feared one. It never initiated a new approach, the dog did nothing new, so it remained the same and never moved on. It feared the next level, having overcome the first obstacle but couldn't go through the second one. As I was watching the dog, then I said to myself, what the dog is doing is a symptom of fear and I discovered this mystery.

At often times we experience what the dog went through. We fear to take risk, we fear to do something new. I found out that, to go where you have never been, you have to pass where you have never passed. The same approach brings the same results and we stay the same. ***"Twenty years from now you will be more disappointed by the things you didn't do than the things you did. So throw off the bowlines. Sail away from the safe harbour. Catch the trade winds in***

your sails. Explore. Dream. Discover" said Mark Twain. There are a lot of great things outside the box, the house or our comfort zone. If you could take the risk and jump out of the moving train that is going nowhere, that contains the poverty, sicknesses, disappointments, stagnation and jump into freedom, we will literally be happy and be very successful. If you're not willing to take a risk and overcome the fear that is stopping you from going to the next level in life, you will be in the same place for five years and for the rest of your life. For about 7 days the dog remained in the same position and never moved out of the situation it was going through because the dog allowed fear to dictate for it. Fear placed a *"stop"* sign whenever it decided to jump and said *"what if you break your leg?"*

Fear Is Necessary

*"Courage is resistance to fear, mastery of fear, not absence of fear." –
Mark Twain*

I want to create a mental picture in your mind that fear is somehow necessary. Fear doesn't mean you don't have to do what you want to do, you will fail or you can't. You should be determined to use fear to turn your life around and achieve all you want. Honestly, I'd urge you to reach the level where you feel fear as a motivating tool beyond your failures, depression and ridiculousness. Look back at your life not to lament over what you have lost, but in a perspective of the things that fear stopped you from. I believe there has been so many things you never tried that could have made you great because you were stopped by *"what if"*. The ideas you never executed which has been executed by someone and you sit back to say *"Oh I had this in mind"* but the unbreakable truth is, you allowed fear of failure to stop you from realizing your dreams, ideas or ambitions.

Take the risk to do whatever the heck you want to do, not thinking about failure but the possibility of you succeeding. Even if you fail, do not fear or attempt to try again. Failing at an attempt doesn't mean you cannot do it, rather you can but have to try again and change your approach. I discovered that most people are afraid of being judged by others and so they never really try for what they really want. They fear the opinion of others which merely shouldn't control their thoughts and beliefs.

Before Donald Trump became the president of the United States of America, I heard Dr. Myles Munroe saying, he happened to meet him in person, when he went to play golf in one of his golf clubs. He has then been successful in Real Estates. He asked Donald Trump *"Sir, please can I ask you a question? If yes, what made you so successful in real estates?"* Not because he wanted to do real estates as well, but because he believed whatever has been his factor it could also help him in his area of specialty. Trump replied *"Failure!"* He went on to say that He failed in his journey to become a real estate mogul, he went bankrupt two times before becoming successful.

Why am I sharing this? To believe in yourself and be successful you have to lose everything first, it has to cost you. He didn't allow the *"what if"* factor to stop him. He invested his money and all were gone. He failed but that was not the end. He used that failure to motivate himself to becoming successful today. He was not limited by fear. I assume if you were to be in his position, you would stop and try something else the first time you failed let alone trying the second time and failing again. You'll say, *"well this is not what am good at."* The fact that you fail at something you try does not mean you were not born to do it or perhaps you're not good at it. People fail a couple of times at things they try and never attempt it again for fear that they will fail again, which is completely wrong. You have to see every failure as a learning stage in your quest to believing in yourself and manifesting greatness.

Understand What Fear Really Is

"Fear is nothing else but a state of mind" – Napoleon Hill

Whenever you try something and you fail, don't see it as a failure, see it as a lesson and will do better in your next attempt. To strengthen your self-believe, you have to bear in mind that, no matter what happens, you will improve from experience. To be strong and brave, you will have to overcome something that frightens you and let go of your ego. Personally, I see fear as a dictator, it dictates the decisions you take and the choices you make and it can only grow louder and stronger if you feed it daily. Brendon Burchard in 'The Motivation Manifesto' wrote ***"Fear rips us from freedom. It is the destroyer of greatness. We know this, and we know we should tame our mind in order to defeat fear."*** When I discovered this, I never allowed my fears to define me.

Basically, fear has to be available for courage to exist. Courage is not the absence of fear. Instead of allowing your fears to defeat you, use it to motivate yourself. It is just an emotion like other emotions. Wrongly, we have pampered fear and allowed it to rule and have dominion than it was created to. Its purpose has been changed and its killing a lot of dreams and ambitions today. Fear was given to us as a motive to avoid physical harm and death and we are the ones who has perverted it into a tool for the ego's protection. Fear is a thief of man's light. No doubt, that this may be a necessary instinct that will cause us to make smart decisions to avoid pain, danger or struggle, but we must be wary of it. To overcome fear we must understand the meaning of fear. Psychologist has proven that as babies we have only two fears; the fear of loud noise and the fear of falling. All other fears are developed as a result of our experiences, they come from what we think or what we hear and see.

Brendon Burchard defines fear as **human motive of aversion**. In my own words and understanding I will define fear as *"a feeling that robs us from greatness."* It doesn't help us to commit to higher aims and imagine greatness. It has become a crutch for emotional weakness. We are afraid of being rejected, isolated or abandoned—not of being chased by a predator. I remember people asking me why am I so confident in public speaking? But they are not good enough for that... I realized that, they are not worried if the audience will attack them physically but rather, they are afraid of failure or maybe making mistakes in their speech.

The Purpose of Fear

Fear is a short-term nature of a motive to avoid a physical harm or danger but has been made a long-term nature to avoid difficult situations. It has made us to seek emotional comfort to avoid failing. Naturally, we all struggle with self-belief, and want to do our best but the great challenge is that in our unconditioned mind, fear is the loudest thing we respond to. We are more alert to the sound of dogs barking than angels singing. In other words, we pay attention to fear than what we desire, our goals. We respond to fear than we respond to our desires and ability to fulfil our dreams. To overcome your fears you have to approach it with curiosity while taking note of your reactions. I also believe by listening closely, you come to understand the language of your fears. If you can understand the language your fear speaks then you can overcome it. Because, the more you know something, the better you can take courage to overcome it. Therefore, if you can identify your fears, you can work progressively to overcome it. You paralyse your fears and silences your doubts when you consider all possibilities and avoid your ego's protection. You can't afford to let your fears keep you down and stifle your greatness. Your life is too big to allow yourself to play too small.

The Curios Criminal

There was a criminal who had committed a crime. He was sent to the king for his punishment. The king told him he had a choice of two punishments. He could be hung by a rope or take what's behind the big, dark, scary, iron door. The criminal quickly decided on the rope. As the noose was being slipped on him, he turned to the king and asked: *"By the way,* (out of curiosity) *what's behind that door?"* The king laughed and said: *"You know, it's funny, I offer everyone the same choice, and nearly everyone picks the rope."* *"So,"* said the criminal, *"Tell me. What's behind the door? I mean, obviously, I won't tell anyone,"* he said, pointing to the noose around his neck. The king paused then answered: *"Freedom, but it seems most people are so afraid of the unknown that they immediately take the rope."*

When I read this story, it left me thinking and I got to know that this is very practical to our lives. Most times when we face a situation we literally come out to say I had no option, now take this; there is always an option in every situation. Clearly the king said that he offers every criminal the same options but everyone opts for the rope because of fear. They think the rope is the easiest and better way to die than to go behind the big, dark, scary, iron door which in disguise is freedom. We all fear something, therefore, you should never be afraid to fear and go beyond where you are. Be ready to take new challenges, take risk and you can control your fear. If the criminal knew that there is freedom behind the iron door he would have opted for that but out of fear he did not hesitate to choose the rope. That is why it is always said ***"The cave you fear to enter, holds the treasure you seek."*** We all seek something but we are afraid to go into the cave to get the treasure we want, we are afraid to go through the storm to get that blessings we seek. We are afraid to go through the challenges and hard times; we are afraid to step out of our comfort zone and get what we want but rather out of fear we stay back and settle for less than we deserve and blend in.

Warren Buffet

If there's a success story that can convince you of the untapped potential of people who overcame fear (of public speaking, doing something, whatever it is you fear), it's the story of Warren Buffett's unbelievably prosperous career. Once a college student who was *"terrified of getting up and saying [his] name,"* Buffett was able to overcome his aversion to speaking in front of others by facing his fears head on. It was not easy, though. He spent much of his college years avoiding courses that would require him to speak in front of the class. At one point, he mustered the courage to sign up for a public speaking course but then dropped out the last minute. At the age of 21, he started his career as a stock broker and realized that he had two choices: either force himself to face his fears or avoid them and never reach his full potential. Buffett finally decided to take the first path and enrolled in a Dale Carnegie course on public speaking. He was relieved to find that there were 30 other people in the class who were experiencing the same anxieties and was able to complete the course. *"You have to do it. And the sooner you do it, the better. It's so much easier to learn the right habits when you're young. If you have a fear of associating with people, you have to go out there and do it, and it's painful...,"* he said in an interview.

Joel Osteen

This world-renowned minister knows a thing or two about putting aside your fears to reach as many people as possible with a message. At the age of 36, he gave his first sermon and recalls being *"scared to death."* Up until that moment, he had felt perfectly comfortable remaining behind the scenes as his father preached week after week. Little did he know that he would have to speak a lot more often in front of thousands of people. When his father passed away, he was encouraged to take over the ministry. But his fear of speaking in public was compounded by the fact that he was compared to his father time and again. It wasn't unusual for him to overhear others saying that he wasn't *"as good as his father."* Osteen decided to put his own teachings into practice and began to re-label himself in his own mind. By ignoring the criticisms and replacing them with positive and encouraging words. He was able to overcome his insecurities and doubts. His positive affirmation techniques seemed to have worked. Today, Osteen heads the largest Protestant church in the US.

You Will Fail—The Untold Truth

"Each failure contains the seed of your next success—if you are willing to learn from it." – Paul Allen

Looking at the sub-heading you will ask yourself; Am I serious? I am aware positivity is what we all run after and preach. But here's a part many don't include in their books and any other inspirational media. You read a lot of books on how to become successful or how to grow your business or church but you hardly find the part of the book when they stab someone in the back, when people say no to you. People turn a leaf out of the dark parts. We're not told that challenges will hit us, troubles will come, and yet we have to move through. So when we get hit hard by challenges, we give up.

Someone tells you a success story and you become pumped up and motivated enough to get to the top. But when you get hit or disappointed, you give up. No! Samuel Buckett said **"Ever tried. Ever failed. No matter. Try Again. Fail again. Fail better."** Failure; the greatest teacher, it builds you. Rocky Balboa also said something I find worth sharing; **"The world ain't all sunshine and rainbows, it's a very mean and nasty place and I don't care how tough you are it will beat you to your knees and keep you there permanently if you let it; you, me or nobody is going to hit as hard as life. But it ain't about how hard you hit, it's about how hard you can get hit and keep moving forward. That's how winning is done."**

We all the time program our minds that things will somehow get better and the road will always be smooth and there will be no storms to distract us or make us park and never continue the journey as we settle for less. But we have to be willing to fight through the storms, to push hard even in the face of failure, get up strong and try again. *"We build failure when we're idle, we overcome it when we take a step." – Richmond George Ahornor*

Listening to an interview; I hardly remember the person but today he is really successful and is celebrated in America. He was asked *"Third failure in a row, did you think you need to park this?"* To my surprise, he replied *"Never"* and the host of the program asked him *"Why not?"* He said something that touched my heart, and it has kept me moving since and always in my mind. He said ***"I don't ever give up."*** How many of us today are willing to say this in the face of failure as I heard this in my heart ***"You may experience many failures but you must not fail to succeed"***.

You must look at failure and tell it straight into the face that *"hey, you keep affecting me but I will never give up until I get what I want."* Every great person you know has experienced failure. ***"Truth be told, every champion, every king, every soldier, every president, every lion, every winner, every victorious person has felt it—the urge to quit. Don't you ever give up on your dream." – Bishop TD Jakes*** Nobody in the world succeeds without failing. So why think of quitting at the point of failure? The great musicians today, once had their demos or mixes rejected by record labels when they were getting started.

Many movie actors and actresses failed at their auditions before climbing to the top. After his first audition, Sidney Poitier was told by the casting director, *"Why don't you stop wasting people's time and go out and become a dishwasher or something?"* It was at that moment, recalls Poitier, that he decided to devote his life to acting. Henry Ford failed and went broke five times before he succeeded.

On listening to a failure story from Rev. Alexander Agyapong he said *"What made me successful today, is the number of times I failed."* Let me also quote Dr. Mensa Otabil, *"Don't stop pursuing your dream because it didn't work out the first or the hundredth time."* The only hindrance to your success tomorrow is your fear of failure today. The number of failures I have encountered is absolutely uncountable—perhaps that has been my greatest motivation to keep striving until I succeed.

Chapter Nine

Your Attitude Counts

"Attitudes are a secret power working twenty-four hours a day, for good or bad. It is of paramount importance that we know how to harness and control this great force." – Irving Berlin

Everyone on earth is unique. If you want to be an impactful personality you have to develop certain types of thinking and perceptions that change the way you see yourself and see the world. The lion is a special animal with the greatest attitude in the animal kingdom. He is the king of the jungle. The lion is not the smartest, heaviest, tallest or biggest animal in the jungle but yet he is the king. Therefore, this rules out all your excuses to believe in yourself and be successful in whatever you seek to do. The lion to me possess a great attitude that makes him the leader. What makes the lion so unique? Is it's attitude. *"An army of sheep led by a lion will always defeat an army of lions led by a sheep – Dr. Myles Munroe.*

Leadership can transform cowards into a violent army, because the lion as a leader has the right kind of attitude that makes him successful in his endeavour. He is the king of the jungle because of his attitude. Your attitude is everything to the success you seek. How do you approach situations and deal with people. Although there are big animals in the animal kingdom, they are all afraid of the small cat. The size is not the problem, the way he thinks makes him act and be successful.

Due to attitude when the elephant, the giraffes, the antelopes, the hippos see the lion what comes in mind is ***the eater*** and other way round when the lion sees the elephant, hippo, or antelope he sees ***"lunch"***. Attitude is everything and makes everything possible. Your attitude produces certain behaviours. Begin to change your mentality to see certain circumstances differently. If you have the right kind of attitude you will see challenges as stepping stones to your success. How do you think? Attitude is defined by the dictionary as *a complex mental state involving beliefs, feelings, values and dispositions to act in certain ways*—by this, your actions or the way you act is being determined by the attitude you possess. You are your attitude and your attitude is you.

Your attitude is something you can never fake. You cannot try to be confident if you're not confident. You cannot try to be loving if you're not loving. In other words, your attitude is more important and powerful than wealth but can also keep you poor. Your attitude is not your appearance but has a lot to do with your actions. The attitude you exhibit creates the first impression you make. It is seen and felt when you make an interaction with something or someone.

Your expression, body language and the tone of your voice exposes your attitude.

Your Attitude Is A Product Of Your Belief System

You can never have an attitude beyond your belief. Your attitude will always stem from your belief system. What makes the lion the king of the jungle is because of what he believes about himself? He believes the elephants and the hippos are lunch and he can eat them and he succeeds in doing that. What do you believe you can do? How do you act towards your beliefs? If you don't like who you are, then you have to change your attitude and what you believe in. Your attitude is developed by the perception of who you are, your existence and your significance on earth—in essence, your self-concept. If you can get these three things to come alive, your attitude will emerge with your greatest ability together with your believe. Your mentality has to be equal to your ability. Belief is so powerful that it can make a hippo to act like a sheep in front of a lion. What you believe about yourself determines the way you think about yourself and the way you think about yourself determines the way you act (attitude).

You should never forget that no one is responsible for your life except you, so you have to make the best out of your life and develop a positive attitude that will help you get all you want in life like the lion. Don't be a hippo or elephant with strength and power and run away from a lion with attitude and belief. You don't need to be big, tall, smart or intelligent, you only need a positive self-belief system which will activate a better attitude. Ability is not everything, attitude and belief is. The elephant and the hippo has the ability, strength and power but what they lack is belief and attitude. What you think is more important than what you do. It is your thinking that influences your actions. Your attitude is like a magnet; it attracts what you express on the outside—if you are positive and loving, people will respond back to you with the same kind of attitude because there is a direct relationship in that.

Imagine there are two people doing the same business on the same stretch of a road. One is more friendly, always smiling and happy whiles the other is unsmiling, not friendly. Which of them are you more likely to buy from? You know your answer. That's the effect the attitude you possess brings into your life. You and I would agree that, a person with a positive attitude can make more progress in a couple of years than a person with a negative attitude could make in ten or twenty years.

The attitude you possess determines the respect you command. If you have the right kind of attitude it commands respect from people. Your age is not a determinant for the kind of respect you will attract. It has less effect on the respect that people gives you. This generation gives respect to people with the right kind of attitude and proves of success. Your belief is a strong contributor to your attitude—because it is what you believe in that programs the attitude you express on the outside. William James once said, that ***"by changing the inner attitudes of your mind which is your beliefs, you can change the outer aspects of your life."*** The attitude you bring to the world, your relationships and all you do in life is very important. It is therefore, a contributing factor which comes from your self-belief.

The Law of Liking

By attitude the lion in the jungle exhibits the law of liking which states; *"The more people like you, the more they will be open to your influence and the more they will help you to achieve your goals."* The other animals in the jungle are moved by the influence of the lion, why? Because he has the right kind of attitude and he is the only animal I have discovered to possess the greatest kind of attitude. The other animals help him achieve his goals and keep his reign as a successful king. A lot of people today have the wrong kind of attitude which creates the wrong impression before people. They fail to influence people and in their endeavours of doing something at heart to them. In an interview with the famous athlete in the world, Cristiano Ronaldo; he was asked *"Are you the best footballer in the world?"* He boldly replied, *"In my mind, I am the best, I don't care about your opinion."* He has the right kind of attitude to who he thinks he is which is very important.

The opinion of others should not determine your attitude and mindset about yourself. Most leaders lack the right kind of attitude and if you are willing to be a great leader, I will urge you to study the attitude of the lion and how he leads in the jungle. You will discover great mysteries that will help you develop the right kind of attitude which in turn, shoot you to the top and make you successful.

Your attitude also attracts relationship. If you possess the right attitude people will love to come to you and be with you. Your attitude serves as an attraction point to your life. You have a great hidden potential and it is your attitude that will attract the right kind of people to help you achieve your goals. It is true that *"your attitude determines your altitude"*. When your attitude place you in a certain altitude, there would be certain level of opportunities that you may enjoy. If you can understand this, the doors of opportunity that has been closed to people will be opened unto you. If you can possess a genuinely positive, optimistic mentality and attitude. *"If you really want to experience a continuous stream of good luck and happy circumstances, you owe it to yourself to develop the kind of personality that radiates warmth and confidence, and which attracts people to you wherever you go." – Brain Tracy.*

I strongly believe, you would agree with me that the most important thing to do is to be mindful of the way you act and take absolute control of your expressions, body language, the way you talk. Make sure you behave and act like the kind of person you want to be. And don't forget that the opinion of people about you is not a factor in you becoming who you want to be. After you exhibit the right kind of attitude to become the person you want to be, you have to connect that to your attributes—thus your inborn abilities or gifts you were born with and the skills you possess. Then you have to build your aptitude—educate yourself on your field of specialty. Become the best in what you do which will create your level of altitude—thus your level of association, the kind of people you meet and mingle with. I call these, *"the 4 A's"*.

The CEO of Your Life

"You're the CEO of your own life, start making executive decisions today." – Stephen Luke

In this sub section, I want to bring to you a powerful idea that struck a chord in me when I first heard it. I believe it can change the perception of your life and get you to take action. Until you realize that everything that happens to you is in your own hands and be responsible for your own actions—you will never believe in yourself. Don't allow anyone to tell you what is possible or not possible, take charge of your life.

I remember having a chat with a friend. I asked her, *"What are your life goals?"* She then opened up on her career path. She said *"The real dream was to become a journalist but I also like fashion. My dad wants me to do nursing and my brother wants me to go to Teachers' Training. I'm confused."* Then I said to her *"Its simple, what do you really want to do that will make you happy?"* She said to me *"Fashion but I am afraid they would not agree with me."* The conversation became interesting after I asked her if I can help. She agreed and I said to her ***"Do not be afraid! You're the CEO of your life. You have to set out to do whatever you want to do and become whatever you want to become. Never allow anyone to stop you from becoming what you really want to become. Have a discussion with your dad and brother and tell them what you want to do. Ask them to believe in it and support you."***

I am convinced she is not the only one facing this kind of confusion with what she wants to do with her life. If you happened to be a parent reading this book. Please, allow your children to become what they want to become. All you have to do is to support and direct. Not to dictate and control. Few friends I spoke to about the same problem told me they cannot decide on their own because they don't own their lives. Their parents are in absolute control because they feed, shelter and pay their fees. If they disobey, they will loose everything.

But this is wrong. I strongly believe if you can find the courage to speak to your parents or whomever is taking care of you. They will understand and come to the realisation that you're in control and you alone know what you have inside you. Therefore, it gives you the mandate to choose what you become.

Being a CEO is not just a special title that is only for the smart or special people. I believe being a CEO has a lot more to do with attitude which goes a long way to affect your belief system. To obtain remarkable results in your life you have to be in control of your life. You have to be at the wheel, set your path right, your purpose and pace. Start making smart decisions in your life. You're the master of your life, the captain of your soul. Never allow the life you have led so far make you believe that you can't live the life you want.

Chapter Ten

The Icons of Self-belief

"The measure of life is not its duration, but its donation."
– Peter Marshall

You will agree with me that some individuals have built good legacies for prosperity because of their efforts and belief they had in themselves. Let's take a look at a few of them, who through self-belief achieved their goals and fulfilled their destiny. Their lives has really been motivating and inspiring. From what they have to go through to be at the top, believing they can and manifesting the greatness they saw. Everything they have achieved through hard work, determination and perseverance was all through the mother factor of self-belief.

Cristiano Ronaldo – Football Athlete (Portugal & Juventus)

Cristiano Ronaldo dos Santos Aveiro born on February 5, 1985, in Funchal, Madeira, Portugal, a small island off the western coast of the country to Maria Dolores dos Santos Aveiro and José Diniz Aveiro. Cristiano has an elder brother, Hugo and two elder sisters, Elma and Liliana Cátia. His name was inspired by the former US-president, Ronald Reagan, whom his father was influenced by. His father was a gardener with the municipality while his mother worked as a cook. Ronaldo was the youngest child among four children. He was raised Catholic in a poor family and grew up in a small house in the city of Funchal and began playing soccer for a youth team in Madeira, where his dad was the team's equipment manager.

Ronaldo was expelled from school after assault on his teacher by throwing a chair at him. He claimed his teacher disrespected him by *"making fun of his Cape Verdean accent and stressing that football would not make him great."* I believe many have had their teachers saying such words to them and affecting their conscience and who they want to be. I know Ronaldo would really be hurt by the words of his teacher and wanted to defend his passion and what he wants to be. If he had listened to his teacher that, football would never make him great, he wouldn't be a legend in the history of football today. Because he never allowed the opinion of his teacher to define his passion and destiny.

He had always been a keen footballer and by the time he was 14 years old he decided to concentrate on becoming a professional footballer. Ronaldo had been playing for Androrinha since he was eight. In 1995, Cristiano Ronaldo joined the club 'Nacional' located in his home town of Madeira and following his good show for them, he joined one of the biggest clubs in Portugal, namely, 'Sporting CP' after clearing a trial. However, in the summer of 2003, when Sporting played against Manchester United and defeated them, Cristiano caught the attention of Manchester United manager, Sir Alex Ferguson. Ronaldo became Manchester United's first-ever Portuguese player. In 2009, Cristiano Ronaldo became the most expensive player in the world after Spanish giant Real Madrid paid Manchester United £80 million to bring him to Madrid and in July 2018 he joined Juventus for €120 million.

He was awarded the Ballon d'Or (later known as the FIFA World Player of the Year Award) in 2008, when he was a Manchester United player. In 2013, he won the FIFA World Player of the Year Award and won it again the following year. He is now a five times Ballon d'Or winner. Cristiano Ronaldo holds the record for being the highest scorer in the history of Real Madrid with 338 goals (as at 2019). Cristiano Ronaldo is the highest ever goal scorer in the UEFA Champions League with 89 career goals as at 2019. Forbes magazine ranked him the world's highest-paid athlete in 2016 and 2017. I cannot put all his achievements and records here because he has a marvellous career and this is just a summary of who he is and his beginning to what he has achieved so far and still counting.

The story and life of the famous footballer is so inspiring and he has been my inspiration and idol since childhood. In an interview he said ***"I've never tried to hide the fact that it is my intention to become the best."*** And now he is truly the best without doubt.

His top ten rules for success states;
- Just play
- Be competitive
- Always take on new challenges
- Know your priorities
- People will judge you
- Work hard
- Believe you're the best (self-belief)
- Play for the team
- Enjoy the moments
- Have a sense of humour

Ronaldo has been very hard working in developing his physics. I remember him saying in an interview that when he was playing for sporting CP, they told him he was very talented but too skinny, he felt the urge to improve on his physics and build a strong and healthy body shape. He did that through hard work, extra training and sacrifice which are ingredients to his success today. I also remember when Manchester United won the UEFA Champions league in 2008, when the team returned to Manchester and everybody was celebrating and going to sleep afterwards, he went to train. Even after being a world champion that night he went to train. Such a remarkable career and would forever be remembered in the history of football and sports.

Brian Tracy – Motivational Public Speaker

Brian was born in Vancouver, Canada on January 5, 1944 to a family that had constant money worries and bills that went unpaid. His dad couldn't hold regular work, so he and his three brothers were used to living with charity clothes and possessing little in the way of luxuries. He dropped out of school early and began a young life of hard, physically demanding work. He left high school when he was 18 without graduating. His first job was a dishwasher in the back of a small hotel. From there, he moved on to washing cars, and then washing floors with a janitorial service. For the next few years, he drifted and worked at various labouring jobs, earning his living by the sweat of his brow. He worked in sawmills and factories. He also worked on farms and ranches. He worked in the tall timber with a chain saw and dug wells when the logging season ended. He even worked as a construction labourer on tall buildings, and as a seaman on a Norwegian Freighter in the North Atlantic.

Most at times he slept in a car, or in cheap rooming houses. When Brian was 23, he was worked as an itinerant farm labourer during the harvest, sleeping on the hay in the barn and eating with the farmer's family. He was uneducated, unskilled, and at the end of the harvest, unemployed once more. He woke up one day and realized, he was the only one who could make himself a success, or a failure, he then set goals and believed he can be successful—he began a sales job; albeit haphazardly: he was a little rough around the edges. But after quizzing other successful sales people and reading profusely, he began making goals and achieve those goals. One such goal was to become the most successful sales person and he pursued it wholeheartedly. He stood upon a set of principles which include *"taking responsibility for your emotions; they can actually be controlled."* And also, **"that you must be crystal clear about the goals you are setting yourself and believe in yourself; don't let your emotions cloud your judgments, or your rash-negative thinking cause you to act ill towards achieving success."**

Today, Brian is a millionaire and a well-respected author of more than 45 books, which have been translated into dozens of languages. Brian Tracy is a 'General of Business Success,' an example of what can be achieved; and a highly sought after conference speaker. His wealth of knowledge and wisdom has been developed over many years; from humble beginnings—being raised in a poor family, to a global leader. Brian has 'walked the road to learning' that countless others dare not tread; and along his way he has created a mass of followers' hungry to learn and succeed themselves.

Misty Copeland - American Ballet Dancer

She was born on September 10, 1982 in Kansas City – Missouri, U.S. Misty Copeland and her siblings grew up with a single mother whose several failed marriages resulted in financial instability. Her first formal encounter with dance was on the drill team of her middle school. The team's coach noticed her talent and recommended that she attend ballet classes taught by Cynthia Bradley at the local Boys & Girls Club. Though age 13 was a late start for a serious dance career. She was rejected because of her age and body type. It was clearly stated that she has the wrong body features for ballet dancing. Unfortunately for her she indirectly suffered from racism; but all these could not break her down.

That was a huge blow but she did not give up on her dream. She did not allow the norms of society or perhaps the facts and measurement of an institution determine whether she can be a ballet dancer. Copeland began taking classes to improve herself and prove society wrong. In 1998, at age 15, she won first prize in the ballet category of the Los Angeles Music Center Spotlight Awards. In 2000 Copeland won another full scholarship, this time to the ABT's intensive summer program. That year she was also named the ABT's National Coca-Cola Scholar. At the end of the summer, she was invited to join the ABT studio company, a selective program for young dancers still in training. Soon after, in 2001, she became a member of the ABT's corps de ballet, the only African American woman in a group of 80 dancers. Though she was challenged by her difference, not only in skin colour but also in body type, always more full-figured than her peers (and regularly reminded), she nevertheless climbed the ranks by virtue of her exceptional skill. In 2007 she became the company's first African American female soloist in two decades.

Copeland's inspiring story made her a role model and a pop icon. She became a strong advocate for diversifying the field of ballet and creating access for dancers of varying racial and economic backgrounds. ***"It's about the journey and enjoying and loving the body you're in now and enjoying the process of getting to wherever you want to go,"*** she said when sharing her story with the students of Harvard.

When I read her story, I was moved, motivated and inspired. How many of us today are willing to be strong and not give up on our dreams. If she had listened to the opinions and rating of others she would have never made a difference and become exceptional. I know many people before her had given up on their dreams because they were rejected and did something else but she was exceptional and created a way for other people like her. She now offers training and mentorship to dance teachers in racially diverse communities around the country as well as in Boys & Girls Clubs.

Lindsey Stirling – American Violinist

Lindsey Stirling was born on 21 September 1986 in Santa Ana, California. She started displaying her interest in music at a tender age. Though her family was a humble one, her parents appointed a violin teacher for her and she started receiving lessons from the early age of five. Lindsey Stirling came to national popularity in 2010 through her appearance in the American reality show 'America's Got Talent', where she managed to impress the judges in the initial rounds by mixing hip-hop, pop, as well as classical music on the violin. She also danced along with playing the violin, something for which she had practiced very hard.

Despite the fact that she performed brilliantly, she was knocked out and failed to move towards the semi-finals. When Lindsey decided to do something different and not just playing violin but dancing and creating movements while playing she was kicked out and her unique style was awfully criticized by the judges as well as many others. But in essence, she continued to embrace it. The judges drastically told her that the movements she was introducing into her style of performance is not making her great as she used to be from the beginning of the competition. They also emphasized on the fact that the movement will make her miss the notes she was playing and will only cause distractions to her performance.

They tried to stop her from being unique, from being what she believed she could do. They tried to talk her out of her goal. Their remarks that day on her performance was very bad, but here's the good news. She later stated in an interview that she only managed to be successful as she had stayed true to herself and believed in what she wanted to do. At often times we quit the seconds we get talked to, the moment someone tells us we suck at something. But if you could embrace that critics and focus on what you're doing and believe in yourself you will be successful at it. Never allow anyone to tell you what you can do or not do.

Today, Lindsey Stirling is a well-known American violinist, dancer, and composer known for works such as her music video 'Crystallize', which became the eighth-most watched video of the year 2012. She has been nominated for eighteen awards over her career so far, out of which she has won ten. Her wins include two Billboard Music Awards, both for Top Dance/Electronic Album, for her albums 'Shatter Me' and 'Brave Enough' in 2015 and 2017 respectively. In 2016, she won the Shorty Awards for Best YouTube Musician.

Mark Zuckerberg – Computer Programmer

He was born on May 14, 1984, in White Plains, New York, into a comfortable, well-educated family, and raised in the nearby village of Dobbs Ferry. He is one of the four children and only son of Karen (née Kempner) and Edward Zuckerberg. His mother is a psychiatrist while his father is a dentist. His three sisters are Randi, Donna and Arielle. They grew up in Dobbs Ferry, New York, in a Reform Jewish household. He is a descendant of immigrants from Germany, Poland, and Austria.

Zuckerberg developed an interest in computers at an early age; when he was about 12, he used Atari BASIC to create a messaging program he named "Zucknet." His father used the program in his dental office, so that the receptionist could inform him of a new patient without yelling across the room. The family also used Zucknet to communicate within the house. Together with his friends, he also created computer games just for fun. *"I had a bunch of friends who were artists,"* he said. *"They'd come over, draw stuff, and I'd build a game out of it."* To keep up with Mark's burgeoning interest in computers, his parents hired private computer tutor David Newman to come to the house once a week and work with Mark. While Mark Zuckerberg was in high school, he landed a job at a company called Intelligent Media Group to develop a music player called Synapse Media Player. He had already garnered a reputation as a programming prodigy when he enrolled in Harvard in 2002.

As part of the class of 2006, he was pursuing degrees in psychology and computer science and was a member of Alpha Epsilon Pi and Kirkland House. During his sophomore year, he developed a program that he named Facemash, which allowed the students to pick the best-looking person from a selection of photographs. After being active during the weekend, Facemash was closed down by Harvard as it clogged one of its network switches and denied many students access to the Internet. There were also complaints from many students about the use of their photographs without their consent. Zuckerberg eventually made a public apology.

In January 2004, he developed the code for his new website. On 4 February, he launched "TheFacebook" from his college dormitory. At first, their service was limited only to Harvard but later Zuckerberg decided to expand it to other schools. In 2004, during his sophomore year, Mark Zuckerberg dropped out of Harvard and subsequently relocated to Silicon Valley. Together with some of his friends, they rented a house in Palo Alto which became their office. By mid-2004, they had already found several investors and moved their base of operation to an actual office. However, they repeatedly thwarted attempts by major corporations to purchase their fledgling company. As Zuckerberg later stated, the mission of Facebook is to make the world open; it was never about the money.

While Mark Zuckerberg was still attending Harvard, he met a biology student named Priscilla Chan at a fraternity party. They started dating sometime in 2003. In September 2010, they moved in together in his rented house in Palo Alto. They married on May 19, 2012, in Zuckerberg's backyard. The occasion also commemorated Chan's graduation from medical school. Chan underwent three miscarriages before giving birth to their daughter, Maxima, in 2015.

In February 2016, the couple announced Maxima's Chinese name, Chen Mingyu. Their second daughter, August, was born in August 2017. In 2010, Mark Zuckerberg was named the Person of the Year by 'Time' magazine. He was awarded CEO of the Year accolade at the 6th annual Crunchies in 2013. In May 2017, several years after dropping out of Harvard, Zuckerberg received an honorary degree from the college at its 366th commencement ceremony. In December 2017, he earned the dubious distinction of being named the recipient of the "Misinformer of the Year" award from the progressive media outlet group, Media Matters. Although Mark was from a humble and comfortable home, he didn't stay in his comfort zone, but he yearned to do more. Right from 12 years he knew his potential and started learning and improving upon himself, his parents gave him the support he needed and they got benefits from it. He faced many challenges through his journey but yet all did not stop him from achieving his greatness and becoming who he believed he wanted to be. Even if you're from a noble home or have some rich parents and you think that will cover you and give you all you want, you deceiving yourself. Develop something on your own so that others will benefit from it. Mark is really an inspiration and a mentor to a lot of people.

Nelson Mandela – Former South African President

Rolihlahla Mandela was born into the Madiba clan in the village of Mvezo, in the Eastern Cape, on 18 July 1918. His mother was Nonqaphi Nosekeni and his father was Nkosi Mphakanyiswa Gadla Mandela, principal counsellor to the Acting King of the Thembu people, Jongintaba Dalindyebo. In 1930, when he was 12 years old, his father died and the young Rolihlahla became a ward of Jongintaba at the Great Place in Mqhekezweni.

Hearing the elders' stories of his ancestors' valour during the wars of resistance, he dreamed also of making his own contribution to the freedom struggle of his people. He attended primary school in Qunu where his teacher, Miss Mdingane, gave him the name Nelson, in accordance with the custom of giving all school children "Christian" names. Mandela began his studies for a Bachelor of Arts degree at the University College of Fort Hare but did not complete the degree there as he was expelled for joining in a student protest. On his return to the Great Place at Mqhekezweni the King was furious and said if he didn't return to Fort Hare he would arrange wives for him. He ran away to Johannesburg instead, arriving there in 1941, there he worked as a mine security officer. He completed his BA through the University of South Africa and went back to Fort Hare for his graduation in 1943. Meanwhile, he began studying for an LLB at the University of the Witwatersrand. By his own admission he was a poor student and left the university in 1952 without graduating. He only started studying again through the University of London after his imprisonment in 1962 but also did not complete that degree.

In 1989, while in the last months of his imprisonment, he obtained an LLB through the University of South Africa. He graduated in absentia at a ceremony in Cape Town. Mandela, while increasingly politically involved from 1942, only joined the African National Congress in 1944 when he helped to form the ANC Youth League (ANCYL). In 1944 he married Evelyn Mase, a nurse. They had two sons and two daughters which the first of whom died in infancy. He and his wife divorced in 1958. Mandela was arrested in a countrywide police swoop on 5 December 1956, which led to the 1956 Treason Trial. Men and women of all races found themselves in the dock in the marathon trial that only ended when the last 28 accused, including Mandela, were acquitted on 29 March 1961.

On 21 March 1960 police killed 69 unarmed people in a protest in Sharpeville against the pass laws. This led to the country's first state of emergency and the banning of the ANC and the Pan Africanist Congress (PAC) on 8 April. Mandela and his colleagues in the Treason Trial were among thousands detained during the state of emergency. During the trial Mandela married a social worker, Winnie Madikizela, on 14 June 1958. They had two daughters, Zenani and Zindziswa. The couple divorced in 1996. On 11 January 1962, using the adopted name David Motsamayi, Mandela secretly left South Africa. He travelled around Africa and visited England to gain support for the armed struggle. He received military training in Morocco and Ethiopia and returned to South Africa in July 1962. He was arrested in a police roadblock outside Howick on 5 August while returning from KwaZulu-Natal, where he had briefed ANC President Chief Albert Luthuli about his trip.

He was charged with leaving the country without a permit and inciting workers to strike. He was convicted and sentenced to five years' imprisonment, which he began serving at the Pretoria Local Prison. On 27 May 1963 he was transferred to Robben Island and returned to Pretoria on 12 June. Within a month police raided Liliesleaf, a secret hideout in Rivonia, Johannesburg, used by ANC and Communist Party activists, and several of his comrades were arrested. On 9 October 1963 Mandela joined 10 others on trial for sabotage in what became known as the Rivonia Trial. While facing the death penalty his words to the court at the end of his famous "Speech from the Dock" on 20 April 1964 became immortalised:

"I have fought against white domination, and I have fought against black domination. I have cherished the ideal of a democratic and free society in which all persons live together in harmony and with equal opportunities. It is an ideal which I hope to live for and to achieve. But if needs be, it is an ideal for which I am prepared to die."

On 11 June 1964 Mandela and seven other accused, were convicted and the next day were sentenced to life imprisonment. Mandela's mother died in 1968 and his eldest son, Thembi, in 1969. He was not allowed to attend their funerals. On 31 March 1982 Mandela was transferred to Pollsmoor Prison in Cape Town with Sisulu, Mhlaba and Mlangeni. Kathrada joined them in October. When he returned to the prison in November 1985 after prostate surgery, Mandela was held alone. Justice Minister Kobie Coetsee visited him in hospital. Later Mandela initiated talks about an ultimate meeting between the apartheid government and the ANC. On 12 August 1988 he was taken to hospital where he was diagnosed with tuberculosis. After more than three months in two hospitals he was transferred on 7 December 1988 to a house at Victor Verster Prison near Paarl where he spent his last 14 months of imprisonment.

He was released from its gates on Sunday 11 February 1990, nine days after the unbanning of the ANC and the PAC and nearly four months after the release of his remaining Rivonia comrades. Throughout his imprisonment he had rejected at least three conditional offers of release. On 10 May 1994 he was inaugurated as South Africa's first democratically elected President. On his 80th birthday in 1998 he married Graça Machel, his third wife. True to his promise, Mandela stepped down in 1999 after one term as President. Believing so much in himself and what he could do for his country he never gave up on what he wanted to do for South Africa. He went to prison continuously, suffered various sickness whiles in prison and also rejected conditional efforts of release because he never wanted to give up on his dream. Nelson Mandela never wavered in his devotion to democracy, equality and learning. Despite terrible provocation, he never answered racism with racism. His life is an inspiration to all who are oppressed and deprived; and to all who are opposed to oppression and deprivation. He died in his home in Johannesburg on 5 December 2013.

Affirmations Exercise

Now is the time for you to learn the secrets of life and create a joyous fulfilling life. How do you feel now? What are your current beliefs and emotions? Life does not suck as people say, it is your thinking and belief that sucks. Don't waste time arguing about your limitations. What you can do or not do. It's a waste of time but rather focus on the things you want, believing you have them and work effortless to attain all you want.

The more you talk about the problem the more you anchor it in place and never get out of it. You have to forget and stop talking about the problem. Focus on working daily towards the elimination of the problem. When you change your thinking process then everything in your life will change. Because the way you think programs your life. Everything around you today was attracted by your mindset. Whatever you are is what you draw to yourself. If you're a negative person you will draw negativity and if you're a positive person you will directly draw positivity. You already have the tool in you to make your life better and achieve all you want. These tools are your thoughts and beliefs.

An affirmation is ***anything you say or think.*** A lot of things we mostly say and think is negative and does not create good experiences for us. If you want to change your life, you have to re-train your thinking and beliefs into positive patterns. Believe in your inborn capabilities to make you successful. You must constantly choose words that will help to either eliminate something in your life or create something new in your life. Every thought you think or word you say is an affirmation and would literally happen to you irrespective of it being a negative or positive confession.

The greatest book ever in the history of man, the Bible, says *"Death and Life are in the power of the tongue, and those who love it will eat its fruit" (Proverbs 89:21).* You are using affirmations every moment whether you know it or not. Your beliefs are merely habitual thinking patterns to unleash your goals. What you want and what you believe you deserve maybe very different. Every complaint, is an affirmation of something you really don't want in your life. Be conscious about the way you think and talk. Our thoughts creates our experiences. Always make the choice to think happy thoughts, believe in yourself and step out boldly today to manifest the greatness in you. *You're phenomenal and I believe in you.*

The Choice Is Yours

"Today, you're one step closer towards your dream, the decision is yours to make." – Richmond George Ahornor

I am very confident that the content of this book has profited you. Even as you have gone through this book of noesis and the mysteries you have discovered. I am very convinced you will not continue to think the same way you thought about your life and how you saw yourself—but you now have a great sense of self-belief, purpose and attitude that you can **"do all things through Christ which strengthens you." (Philippians: 4:13)** I am also without doubt, you have dealt with intimidation, opinion of others and inferiority complex. All Glory be to God! The icons of self-belief or perhaps the great achievers of society that were mentioned and discussed in the chapters were not for entertainment or fun but to motivate and inspire you that, regardless of your scope of environment, whether you are from a poor home or affluent home, black or white, whether you are physically challenged or you are strong, living abroad or in your motherland—you can still be great. These great people also lived a life of good morals. In essence, as you yearn for greatness, it calls for you to avoid any form or immorality and follow good morals. ***"With each choice you make, you create your life." – Rev. Alexander Agyapong***

I strongly believe from now and even to the end of your life and in the life of your descendants, you will continue to walk in the fullness of every being you have been designed for as you attach diligence to your efforts. Remember, you cannot remain unchanged after reading this book. If you do, then you would have wasted your time but of course, I am very optimistic that you are going to work towards greatness.

Reminding us once more from our discovery, don't forget we started with the concept of self-belief. We continued with the meaning of self and belief so that we can have a better understanding of the main subject. Then we looked at building our abilities, discovering the differences between fixed and growth belief or mindset. I then spoke about what I went through using my life as an example.

We also discovered the importance of discovering and unleashing our potential. The essence of time and the top five questions that you must answer about yourself to give you a better objective of how to live your life on earth. I hope you haven't forgotten the fact that, one positive relationship with someone at the right moment can initiate a breakthrough in your life or business that will change your life. In the opposite direction, the same relationship with someone can also initiate a problem or a setback in your life or business that will affect you for the rest of your life.

We exposed the hidden thief of our light, which is fear—the great usurper of progress and self-belief. It was also realized that, attitude counts. It is everything and makes everything possible with emphasis from the attitude of the lion. You were again introduced to some important personalities in our time who through the same process of achieving greatness, made it.

It is my fervent prayer for you that the Almighty God will keep you, provide you with all the strength and might to excel in your quest for greatness and fulfilling your divine given destiny. Now step out bold with your shoulders and head raised high and prove your worth.

I believe in you.